THE MYSTERY OF THE GLOW

Bunny Carmean

The Mystery of the Glow
Copyright 2014 by Bunny Carmean

The plot and major characters are fictitious, but the setting of Cape Coral, Florida, is as realistic as possible. The problems are all too real.

All rights reserved. No part of this book may be reproduced, stored in a retrieval system or transmitted in any form or by any means without written permission of the author, excepting brief quotes used in reviews.

ISBN: 1500189391
ISBN 13: 9781500189396

Printed by CreateSpace, An Amazon.com Company

"You miss 100 percent of the shots you never take."
Wayne Gretzky.

This Book's For You

- If you like humor or soccer, you'll get a kick out of this book.
- If nature talks to you, you'll learn what to say back.
- If you live in Cape Coral, Florida, it will be a bonus because this story is about your home.

Prologue

The CHIP was gone.

It had vanished.

The gallium arsenide computer chip, ten times more powerful than any ever known, was put on a space capsule and launched from the Kennedy Space Center.

The mission: to contact life in space using a sound-activated system.

But problems developed.

It whirled radioactive and out of control!

It smashed into a million eerie, glowing pieces and crashed into the Crystal River on Florida's west coast.

Scientists examined the debris.

But they couldn't find the CHIP.

As they frantically searched the Crystal River area on the north side of Buzzard Island on Kings Bay, a fifteen foot fluorescent glow slowly moved through the water on the south side.

And that's where this story begins.

It takes place in Cape Coral, Florida, which is a couple hundred miles south of the crash site. It happens to a teen named J. R. Collins.

CHAPTER ONE

The Invention

It started with a big fight.

Not the kind of fight when kids skip lunch and rush to the playground to watch you and some jerk fight it out. They don't care if you win, lose, or get suspended; those kids cheer because they're personally bored and want a show.

Not the kind of match in a boxing ring where a trainer slides silly looking gloves on your hands like you're unable to dress yourself. Then you end up punchy with a split eyebrow because a referee can't count as high as ten.

It was worse than all that.

It was a fight with my best friend Twinks. Imagine me—J. R. Collins—fighting with Twinks after all these years.

We were at the Pelican Soccer Field—we practically lived there. When we weren't playing soccer on the Cyclones, we field tested our inventions.

Once, Twinks and I created a soccer ball that called out each team member's name. Another time we built a ball that lit up; it was great in total darkness. My favorite was a soccer ball that yelled "goalllllll" every time it entered the net. So rad.

We designed soccer shoes that counted the number of touches on the ball. A robot that carried our soccer equipment. A special hat for practicing head balls.

Twinks and I also worked on high tech stuff.

We built a drone.

Created a virtual reality game or two.

On the day of our argument, we were working on a VR game called *King: for the Goalie Who Rules*. We called it *King* for short. Since I am the tester, I slipped on the virtual reality mask and the special gloves with electronic sensors.

Immediately, it looked like a 3-dimensional soccer field with me in the net as goalkeeper. The forest green, lined field that spread out in front of the goal was so vivid that I pictured the smell of freshly cut grass. Black and white soccer balls were carefully lined up. One by one, the players dashed up and forcefully shot them directly at me.

The Mystery of the Glow

The images and sounds felt so real in there that it actually hurt as dozens of balls slammed me.

THUMP!

Darting wildly, I punched one and volleyed another.

WAM!

I shuffled side to side, closing the angles on each shot, but all my good positioning and mental toughness didn't help. Soccer balls just kept coming.

THUMP!

I slapped one down.

Then another.

THUD!

SLAM!

For over an hour, kids struck soccer balls over and over, pounding me like rockets. They used the instep sweet spot for maximum power. Some shots even went through my legs, megging me. It was so real I forgot I was inside a VR game.

I was out of breath and sweating. Ouch! It hurt! My shoulder throbbed, muscles cramped, and head ached.

One kick was a ball bending into the upper ninety. I flew through the air with all of my might, attempting to block it. I couldn't see Twinks outside the VR game, but I heard him howl, "Don't dive in that direction; there's mud over there!"

Too late. I crashed in the muck. Splash.

Mud. Yuk!

Slop covered me from head to toe. It oozed out of my shirt, across my tongue, and up my nose, stealing my breath. I couldn't see myself, but I bet that when I took the googles off, I would look like a raccoon with big, white eyes.

Then I tried to flip off the mask; I yanked and yanked, but it wouldn't come off. Globs of my own blonde hair jerked out, but I couldn't get the goggles off. I was stuck *inside* the mask. Trapped inside the virtual reality game we had invented. A game so real, you'd swear you were getting slammed by balls.

"Twinks, get this mask off me!" I was mad.

"Stay in the mask a little longer," Twinks called. "You look hilarious. Don't 'mask' your feelings."

It was a Twinks' pun. Whenever he wanted things to lighten up, he'd say puns or knock-knock jokes.

"Maybe it's a riot to watch from out there, but in here it hurts!" I growled.

"Talk about throwing yourself into your work. Did you have a ball?" he chuckled.

As Twinks yanked the virtual reality mask off my eyes, he doubled over with laughter. His dark eyes sparkled as he shoved back his black, curly hair and said, "If you feel lousy, I'll get the medicine ball."

"Twinks, that was like being in a bad dream when you keep doing something over and over and just want to wake up."

He squatted down and said, "Relax. *King* just needs a little work. I'll have it fixed in a jiff."

"Well, they don't call you Twinkletoes for nothing," I said, spitting out mud. Fans call him that because he's the best forward in the state and twinkles the ball faster than anyone, like he has gloves on his feet.

I also call him that because he's a genius on wheels, and our game is cool and should sell like hot cakes. After all, way over two thousand kids sign up with the Cape Coral Soccer Association every year, and they'll buy it.

"We'll finish this VR game tomorrow," I said.

"Can't. Got a new invention," Twinks answered.

"New?"

"Off the hook. I'm hooking an underwater microphone to a computer to test the water quality and listen to dolphins," he said.

"Dolphins? What a bore. Count me out."

"I planned it on 'porpoise' for our science fair project."

"Even if it is on purpose, leave me out. You know I hate water stuff," I said, turning to leave.

"Knock. Knock." (Brace yourself. Here comes a Twinks' joke.)

"Who's there?" I asked.

"Scott."

"Scott who?" I wondered.

"Scott to be a way to get J. R. to work on an underwater invention," Twinks said, grinning.

"Never!" I shouted, flinging my muddy shirt down on the field.

This was the only fight we ever had. Little did I realize it would change my life.

As I got to the parking lot, I yelled back over my shoulder, "Who cares? Ain't anything special in the water anyway."

As J.R. spoke, a couple hundred miles north of Cape Coral, a fifteen foot fluorescent glow was moving away from the island and down the Crystal River.

THE MESSAGE

I woke up for school the next day, feeling like a soccer ball with no air in it. It was the first time Twinks and I ever fought over an invention.

We met at the Pelican Field in the Lollipop League which has soccer drills for four year olds. I had no idea about the soccer part when I signed up, but I figured if someone besides the lady at the bank wants to give me lollipops, I'm all in.

When I first spotted Twinks, he was jumping over small hurdles; he looked like a kangaroo making exact jumps. We learned to dribble in a game called Sharks and Minnows. Twinks and I loved being the sharks because we got to chase all the minnows. When the drills were done, we raced to see who could pick up the most cones for the coach.

Twinks and I got close in kindergarten, and we made up whistles in code. In first grade, they put us in separate classes because the kindergarten teacher said we were a bad influence on each other. By second grade, they put us back together.

Over the years, we got talked out of only one invention—a soccer ball app that told your every move so a coach could use it to train you. People said it was farfetched. You know what? I read a basketball is coming out some day that does the same thing.

There's a lesson there: fight for your dreams.

Our latest creation? A drone.

We figured a plane with no pilot is a hoot. Besides, I read that Amazon wants to deliver packages and Domino wants to deliver pizzas using drones. Drones can be used to find lost people, farm, and count manatees. Ours is remote controlled with a spotlight and a camera for taking pictures of the soccer fields.

Picturing all we had done together, I just couldn't believe Twinks and I had a fight.

Slumping in front of the bathroom mirror, I stared into my own blue eyes, thinking, *Twinks knows I hate water. Besides, maybe technology and the environment can't even exist together.*

I popped in my contact lenses and scuffed to the kitchen, threw together a peanut butter sandwich, shoved it down my throat, and picked up my phone to listen to the messages.

The first message began. "J. R., this is Mom. I'm out of town."

Her voice was flat, and I've learned you don't always know what she's thinking.

Once, when I was little, I had a bad fever that lasted for days. She was always at my side, holding my head, even when I threw up ten times. It was so bad that only mom would stay in the room.

When I stopped, what do you think she did? She started laughing. Finally, weak as I was, I joined her, and we roared until we collapsed. Inside we weren't happy, but that's how it went.

The second message started, "J. R.? Dad here."

Dad is the opposite. Usually he runs smooth, calm, and deep, but I have seen a few exceptions. One time, when I went to his military reunion, I got a different picture of him. As each guy told story after story, Dad laughed and laughed. I never saw him laugh so hard.

We had a long trip home, so we left first. I stretched across the back seat as we drove, and when we were almost home, I glanced at him in the car mirror and saw tears in his eyes.

Dad's message continued, "I'll be late. Grab a bite and clean the pool." Clean the pool? Why me? He knows I never use it.

There was one more message. Since it was from an unlisted number, I figured it was from someone I didn't know. I hoped it would bring some excitement to my life.

"Hammer? You there? Pick up. It's me, Sparrow. We better not get caught doing all this stuff, or we're gonna get in trouble. I'll be right over to talk."

Big thrill. It wasn't even for me. Just a jerk who dialed the wrong number. Dialed me, thinking he was calling some guy named Hammer.

I listened again. *Weird*, I thought.

I was so distracted that I almost left my homework on the kitchen counter. It was about metaphors. On the way out of class yesterday, Twinks said to me, "What's a metaphor? That's where horses live–that's what a meadow's for."

That's a typical Twinks' joke.

Our homework was to write a metaphor comparing life to a concrete object. My teacher Mrs. Green showed us a picture of a train that said life is a train because you must stay on the track.

The kid next to me sketched a box of chocolates, saying he got the idea from a movie.

I sat in class and doodled a roller coaster since they're fun to draw and wrote, "Life is a roller coaster," but I couldn't think of any way to compare the two.

Now, as I grabbed my homework, a marker, and my lunch from the counter and started for school, I got an idea and finished my homework on my way out the door.

"Life is a roller coaster; it has its ups and downs."

The fluorescent glow moved down the river.

SURPRISE AT SCHOOL

Getting to school in record time, I chased Twinks down the hall to the broken water fountain that never turned off. I told him about the phone call and how some guy left a screwy message by mistake.

"You say the guy's name was Sparrow? Calling Hammer? Sounds like cartoon characters. Hey, if our VR game doesn't work, we'll take a hammer to it," Twinks said, motioning like he was picking me up and hammering.

I doubled over with laughter.

Twinks went on. "Knock. Knock."

"Who's there?" I asked.

"One. Two."

"One Two who?" I wondered.

"One two take ole Hammer and pound our project? Well, you don't have to because I already fixed our game with my 3-D printer," Twinks laughed. "I nailed it."

"You're not mad?"

"Me? Never. SOOF," he said, grinning. It was one of the things I like most about him—he's the kind of friend who knows the worst about you and still likes you.

Twinks Cline has always been there *with* me. We taught each other how to ride a bike, a skateboard, and play chess. We built a tree house, played hide and seek with my dog Shadow, had a band, gave magic shows, and went to church together.

He also has been there *for* me. He limped two miles on a bad ankle to watch my All Star game. We were losing when he showed up until I made the best goal of my life for him.

When my granny was in hospice, she was very sick and never even knew who was with her. Yet, Twinks sat in there with me day and night, and that wasn't easy because the room smelled like weird perfume.

When Shadow got hit by a car while playing Frisbee with the girl next door, Twinks weaved through heavy traffic, stopped the cars, and lovingly carried him to my mom. He helped me nurse my beloved dog through the operation and personally built an invention to help Shadow cope until he got used to balancing on three legs.

I always tell Twinks that he's my guardian angel.

As I stood thinking about how much Twinks means to me, I leaned over the fountain and gulped a sip; the water tasted lukewarm and smelled like chlorine. I took a look. Pink gum was smashed on the bottom, looking stuck in place and drowning.

Then kids poured down the hall.

There are four kinds of kids in our school. The ones who run the place—jocks, stars, smart ones. Then the wannabes who hang on to the popular kids every word. Next, those who follow a leader who is some jerk with more muscle than brain. And the invisibles. It's like they aren't even there. No one even says hi to them.

Not me. I always say hi.

Twinks and me? We're in a class all our own. Everyone knows we do our own thing and that he is both sides of the moon.

As Twinks fooled around, the bell to class clanged. The weirdest thing happened. None of the kids went to class. They gathered like when a fight is starting, or some kids are up to no good. The crowd seemed bigger than at the World Cup.

The bell rang again. I knew I'd be in trouble if I didn't get right to class.

I slipped down the hall to see what the crowd was.

As I turned the corner, I saw why all the kids were in the hall. Nicci was back. She smiled and said, "Hi, J. R., you haven't changed this past year."

Maybe I hadn't, but she certainly had. Her shiny, chestnut hair fell to her shoulders; her green eyes sparkled. Excitement filled the air as everyone welcomed her back simultaneously and pledged their votes.

"Yeah. We'll vote for you. Why not? You're the smartest kid in school."

"I'm running for class president," Nicci said, peering directly at me.

A couple kids nudged me aside to get closer to Nicci. "Wow! Some gadget," they said. "You invented it? Awesome."

I watched Nicci sitting straight and proud and tall, nodding at the group. I looked at her wheelchair. It *was* Nicci. Clever. Creative. James Bond-like. She had spent hours on it. Battery powered. Self-propelled. At button touch were a hair dryer, rear view mirror, tiny T. V., and a mini cooler.

I had to give her credit. After months of therapy, here she was back in full swing and even running for president.

Nicci moved through the crowd to me. "Hi, J. R. Thanks for the cards and notes."

"I have to admit you were hard to track down," I said.

"Different treatments."

"Sorry about the accident," I said.

"I know. But it's behind me now. Will you help me campaign?"

"Sure." As I spoke, I was slammed to the side.

The crowd of kids parted as if sliced apart by a sharp knife. Everyone slid back from the wheelchair and me. Buck—tall, broad shouldered with steel grey eyes and pitch black hair—cut his way through with his friends closely following him like a long tail.

"Nicci. Whassssup?" Buck asked in a cold, impersonal way as silence crashed over the area.

"Not much, Buck. You?"

"Not much." He pulled out his comb, dragged it through his hair, and gave it a puff and a pat.

The late bell clanged. Buck muscled his way through the crowd, scraping past me, staring deeply into my eyeballs with his piercing, mean, cold eyes.

At that very moment, the mysterious glow moved into the Gulf of Mexico and started south towards Cape Coral.

CHAPTER TWO

The Threat

For hours I worked on Nicci's election. Campaign banners dangled across my room like a huge New Year's party. As I painted a sign, I got madder and madder, thinking about Nicci saying she couldn't come over to help me.

Finally, I decided to go out and think it through. Jogging along, I thought how much my life had changed lately because of Nicci. And because of Buck. Was that an accidental trip in the hall? Why did he sit on my lunch?

What makes matters worse is that whatever Buck did, all his friends copied. If he wore his hat backward, so did they. If he flexed his muscles, seven other kids looked like it was a Mr. America contest.

After an hour, I returned home. Reaching for the door knob, I spied a note tacked to the door. I ripped

The Mystery of the Glow

it off and tore it open. Someone had cut words out of a magazine and taped them to cardboard. "YOU'VE BEEN WARNED. Stay out of our business!"

I was stunned. I had never gotten anything like that before. *Who warned me?* I stood there, knees shaking, then slowly crept inside.

I was surprised to see a message left on my phone by someone who had blocked their phone number. It was a twisted, disguised voice that sounded like a frog with a cold, straining to speak through a handkerchief. Plugging one ear, I decoded the message, "Meet me noon tomorrow at the Power and Light Company. Come by boat."

The voice sounded slightly familiar. *Who? Who?* The only strange voice I had heard lately was from some guy named Sparrow. Could he be the one threatening me?

Quickly, I texted Twinks who was surprised that Sparrow called and said we could use his dad's boat, pretend to be tourists, and meet Sparrow. It took Twinks fifteen minutes to convince me to go by boat since I hate all that water surrounding me.

Then he sent a text saying he had finished his underwater invention.

"Your dumb idea won't take us anywhere. Boring," I texted back.

"It works, J.R."

"My life's in danger and that's all you can think of?" My stomach was starting to ache.

"J.R., nothing's going to hurt you."

"Time will tell."

LOOKING FOR TROUBLE

The next day we loaded Twinks' boat and started out toward our destiny.

I knew Twinks saw the fight or flight look in my eyes. As he steered up the river under two Cape bridges, he got me to chill out by reassuring me that Sparrow wouldn't show and promising I wouldn't get wet.

Trying to get my mind off of all the water surrounding me, I scanned the Edison Winter Estate. Weird, but that place can help me forget anything.

Gosh, Edison was pure genius. He worked on the incandescent light bulb and moving pictures, and he patented over a thousand inventions.

Suddenly, the brilliant Edison was shoved out of my mind as I pictured Sparrow and Hammer. *How could the same world create such different people?*

I calmed myself and forced my mind off of bad things.

Once, Twinks and I did our book report on Edison. When he invented the phonograph (think today's CD) in 1877, he used a hand-cranked cylinder and said, "Mary had a little lamb," testing if his voice would play back. That cracked me up. Imagine a famous man saying "Mary had a little lamb."

The funniest part of our report was Edison as a kid. At four he tried to make his friend fly, and Tom also sat on goose eggs. I coaxed Twinks to sit on eggs during our speech, but he nixed the idea. Too bad. I think that would have guaranteed an *A* after the kids all stopped clucking.

My mind returned to the present as I watched Twinks navigate some jet skis crossing the wake behind our boat. Staring at the water made me so tense that I decided to shut my eyes, listen to the engine hum, and daydream some more.

When I opened my eyes, we were at the Orange River near the Lee County Power and Light Plant. Twinks anchored near the huge red and white striped towers and we sat, waited, and watched the boats pass. As we scanned the area for Hammer, we pretended to be tourists taking pictures.

The whole thing got on my nerves, but Twinks strutted across the bow like he was under a spotlight telling jokes.

"Knock. Knock," he said.

"Who's there?" I asked, trying to pass time.

"Stepfather."

"Stepfather who?"

"Stepfather one more step and I'll fall off the boat," Twinks said as he took some steps, flailed his arms, and pretended to fall in.

"Then don't step farther," I warned.

Without hesitation, he said, "Knock. Knock."

(Hope you're ready for another one.)

"Who's there?" I asked.

"Police."

"Police who?" I went along with the silly game.

"Police look for Hammer and Sparrow," he said.

"Please look? I am looking. Cut it out, Twinks. I have a headache. They'll be here. Why else would Sparrow disguise his voice? You saw the note," I whined.

"Nothing here but manatees," Twinks calmly said.

"Is that what I see?"

"They're mammals, so when it's cold, they come to the plant's discharge water to stay warm," he explained.

"You mean those flat, smooth circles in the water are from manatees?" I asked.

"Yup. They're hard to see."

I looked closer. The river bubbled with manatees. Hairy, potato-like snouts popped through the water, and an occasional tail splashed, creating the smooth, circular patterns. Bubbles broke the surface as they pulled up grass roots, disturbing the brown, cloudy bottom.

"They're hard to see, all right," I said.

"That's why there are so many no-wake signs with slow speeds. People must drive carefully because boats kill almost a hundred manatees a year in Florida."

"Who cares?" I mumbled.

"They're endangered after being around for 45 million years, for Pete sake," Twinks said.

"Who cares? They look like a bunch of coconuts. We're wasting time on those dumb things. We should be looking out there—for trouble."

PUTT PUTT

After hours of waiting for Sparrow, we pulled anchor and left. "I guess I was wrong about him showing up," I told Twinks.

We went through the no-wake zone under the Fort Myers Bridge. As we putted through, a red cigarette boat zoomed by, nearly shoving us into the pilings. It was Buck and some kids!

"Hey, Putt-Putt, can't you drive that tub any slower? Clean up your act, or we'll clean it for you," Buck sneered as they circled our boat.

They got closer and closer until they soaked us. My face drained, I couldn't breathe, and the voice in my head screamed scary things about water and about me falling into it. I tried to talk back, but I know the voice always wins.

They circled and sprayed us again. The salt water stung my eyes, and I coughed and choked as it poured into my mouth. Drenched and dizzy, I nearly fell overboard.

This definitely wasn't the way a kid so scared of water wants to spend his day.

My head wanted to explode, and I thought my ears were about to pop off from the loud engine roar of

Buck's boat, but that wasn't the worst part. Our boat was flooded, but that wasn't the worst part.

The worst part was seeing Twinks so waterlogged that no one would recognize him. When our eyes locked, Twinks and I were rattled and knew we had to pull each other through it. Not that we had any time to talk it over, or even think, because Buck started screaming threats again.

"Hope you enjoyed the showers. Don't forget to wash behind your ears. Oh, and don't worry about paying for the boat wash; it's one of our free services. See you next week in class if you swim home," Buck yelled in his rough, rumbling voice.

Buck was acting like a big bully because that is the only thing he knows how to do.

They raced their boat up one side of the river and down the other, nearly crashing into a no-wake sign. "No wake. Guys, this is a no-wake zone. Me? I'm awake. Are you, J. R.?" Buck mocked. "Too bad you wasted your day. This is why I called you—to give you a shower."

"Called?" I gulped. "Twinks, the disguised voice was Buck's!"

As I spoke, Buck dragged his comb through his hair, and his boatload of hooting fools turned back toward Cape Coral.

Buck definitely has anger issues, I thought as Twinks and I calmed ourselves, sopped up the water, and got his boat ready to start home.

"Twinks, Buck could join the circus with that act of his. What will I do with all of his friends after me?" I said while still drying off.

"You're about to find out! There they are again!" Twinks exclaimed. It was Buck and friends.

"It's Putt-Putt," Buck yelled. "Get them."

As they chased us, they hit something in the river—like a log. Buck, perched on the front of the boat, somersaulted and crashed into the water.

"What did we hit?" a guy yelled.

"Who cares? We can get them anytime, and I always get even. Come back and get me!" Buck demanded as he bobbed in the water with his wet, flattened hair drooping over his eyes.

I breathed a huge sigh as we escaped. "I wonder what they hit, Twinks."

"I've no idea."

Looking back, we saw them pluck drenched Buck out of the water, jump up and down, and throw cans at us as they zigzagged through the water.

We were all too busy to look in the river. If we had, we would have seen a huge, fluorescent glow moving away from Buck's boat.

CHAPTER THREE

The Meeting

The next day I heard "pop, pow, bam" as I dragged myself past the Cape Coral Yacht Club racquetball courts. The bright green Monk Parakeets crammed in a towering palm tree were squawking, reminding me of all the chatter going on in my head.

I was a drum without a parade.

How could all of this be happening to me?

I plodded past the bike racks and tiki hut to the long pier that extends about 250 yards out over the Caloosahatchee River. Before I stepped on the pier, I peered at the playground to see if anyone was still near the slides spying on me, but all I saw was a bunch of little kids. Then, I stared out at the water and saw the strangest sight.

A crabber tending his traps went past shore with a boatload of pelicans. They were on every row of passenger seats, on the floor, the boat's roof, flying behind, and drifting in the wake of his boat. He was like a taxi driver picking up pelican customers along the way.

He reminded me of Buck and friends.

Giving one final check of the playground to see if anyone was tailing me, I decided the coast was clear and started out on the pier. As I trudged out, a dolphin swam by, and I watched some people fishing over the rail, catching stingrays and catfish. One snagged a sheepshead fish with human-like teeth that looked like it was grinning at me.

A guy hooked a huge fish that dragged him the entire length of the dock until he finally pulled it in. Everyone on the deck rushed over to look at it; it was the largest snook we had ever seen. The man released it.

I wondered if Buck and friends would release me.

Beneath the small, tin roofed shelter at the end of the pier, Twinks had spread out his computer project on a couple benches. He was testing water samples and recording sounds.

"How can you work on this dumb project with all the lousy problems I have?" I asked him.

"Buck? He has a short attention span. He'll forget," Twinks answered.

"Can't you picture those guys throwing cans and swearing? And what about the note? The phone call? To top it off, someone's following me," I said.

"Following you?" Twinks asked.

"Two or three times I spotted someone crouching behind the big cement grill over by the playground watching me. Frankly, I'm not in the mood."

"J.R., you sure you're not getting carried away again?"

"No. Something strange is going to happen," I answered.

"I feel the same. What?" he said.

"Maybe it's about Nicci. She's going to have a victory party, and she told me not to come. After all I did for her campaign! Winning has changed her," I said.

"Nicci will always be the same," Twinks said.

Then he added a knock-knock, and I asked, "Who's there?"

"Scott."

"Scott who?" I asked.

"Scott to be an answer for all of this," Twinks answered.

"There's got to be an answer; I just wish I knew what it was." As I spoke, I saw it! It was the third time I saw it–a baseball cap. Someone wearing a Mike Greenwell baseball cap was slithering through the shadows by the fountain at the end of the pier and staring at us.

"Twinks, look over there," I screamed. "There's the guy who's tailing me."

"Where?"

By the time Twinks looked, the guy with the hat had disappeared.

"I think it's Hammer. Whoever it is slouches and keeps far away."

Twinks and I sneaked along the pier, looking for a guy in a baseball hat. When we got to the other end, no one was there.

I could barely search before Twinks saw it. He yelled out and looked like his eyeballs were going to explode out of his skull. "J.R., look at that!" he screamed, sprinting away from me.

We both forgot about the man in the cap as we stampeded down the pier.

"Look at the computer!" Twinks shrieked.

I saw it too. The audio clicked like a machine gun, and red letters vibrated on the screen.

"I've never seen anything like this before," Twinks noted.

"Me neither. Something is trying to reach us."

"Type," he ordered me.

I frantically pressed the keys. There was no response. "This is crazy," I said.

"What did you type?"

"I told whatever it was that we were 'man'," I said.

"Maybe it's smart enough to know man is often the enemy," Twinks said.

We kept working.

Finally, Twinks nearly fainted as he pointed at the monitor as marks zigzagged across it. A circle appeared. Then a wavy line, shaped like a reversed *S*, cut the circle in half, and a dot plopped on each side of it.

"It sent us a message. What does it mean?"

"How would I know?" I answered. "I typed the word 'man' and it sent this symbol back to me."

"Ask it to explain," Twinks said.

I asked and waited. There was no answer.

A letter appeared on the screen. *M*...

Then *O*.

N...

Y.

I guessed how to pronounce the letters. "Moan-y," I said. "Like in the word 'moan.' "

The screen went blank. Nothing happened. After a few minutes, it tried again and sent up the letters, "R. MONY."

"Its name!" I exclaimed.

"Find out more," Twinks urged.

"What are you?" I asked over and over.

We waited for hours and no other message. I finally said, "We can't reach it again."

"Even if we can't, we've done it!" Twinks exclaimed.

Eyes burning, I motioned, zombie like, for Twinks to shut off the equipment. As he reached for the controls, another line appeared. I shoved his hand away. Slowly, letters floated across the screen.

"Good night!"

TAKE ACTION

Day after day, we tried to contact R. Mony again. Twinks was surprised at my interest since I hate water stuff, but I explained this was different than I expected. This was an unknown creature. Maybe from Mars. This would make us famous.

We went to the yacht club every day and tried to contact the monster.

"Do you think it wants to tell us anything special?" Twinks asked.

"Like what?" I wondered.

"Its secret. Its reason for being," he said.

"Don't read so much into it, Twinks."

We typed on the computer, "R. Mony, come in."

"In where?" Red marks flashed across the screen.

"Are you there?" we asked.

"So far," the mysterious being answered.

We jumped up and down and high fived. "It's answering."

We typed, "What's your message?"

"Message?"

"Yes. If there was one thing to tell us, what would it be?" we wondered.

"Take action," R. Mony answered.

"That's it?"

"That's it for now. What's your message?" the strange, unknown thing asked.

"Ours? We don't even have one. We're just glad to meet you and hope you stay around."

"So do I," the mysterious creature under the water answered, and the screen went blank.

"What strange answers," Twinks said as we cleaned up the equipment. "What do you think it means?"

"How would I know?" I whined. "None of it makes sense to me. But I do wonder what's down there and why it came to us of all people."

Why us?

The glow remained at the Cape Coral Yacht Club as if it had a reason for staying there.

CHAPTER FOUR

Emergency

Twinks and I spent hours texting each other about R. Mony. We didn't understand the strange messages or the puzzling name, but Twinks didn't care about the details; he was just thrilled the computer system worked.

Finally, Twinks signed off texting, so I plunged into cleaning my room. I think I actually needed a shovel, but I dug in by hand. As I cleared off a bookshelf for the DVD's, CD's, and video games, I discovered an old photo album.

I leaned on my elbows and thumbed through my baby pictures. Shot after shot of me with Mom and Dad. Tears splashed on my favorite shot of both parents holding my hands and swinging me over the ocean waves, pretending they were going to throw me to the wind.

The Mystery of the Glow

I hate their divorce, I thought. I've tried to figure out their divorce, but all I see is a storm at sea and I'm a boat, and if I take on any more water, I'll sink.

Last year my cousin had an accident. A bunch of cars were going too fast and tailgating. One car braked, the others piled on, and my uncle crashed to the side of the road, rolling over and over.

Later, my cousin and I talked on the phone, and she told me that her life had passed before her eyes.

That got to me. How could your life pass before your eyes? I've tried to do it. All I get are random snapshots.

Mom loves animals; Dad's a gadget man.

Mom plays tennis; Dad's into soccer.

Sometimes they fight over money.

Dad likes fine restaurants; Mom camps.

He's a mountain; she's an island.

When I was a little kid, it was the three of us. Three peas in a pod. Then it changed. Weeds started growing in our garden. We weren't always all together because someone was always working.

Dad's a home guy; Mom travels.

It always fell to me to smooth things out. With a joke. With perfectionism.

Random snapshots.

Random pieces.

Twinks told me that things at home change no matter what because we're not little kids anymore, and we're becoming more independent. But I don't know about all that.

Where is the piece that explains it all?

And my guilt. Especially the guilt.

I hate their divorce.

Take action. R Mony's words echoed in the back corners of my mind, haunting me like ghosts playing games.

I knew what I had to do. I changed the outgoing message on my phone. I erased the regular one that said, "At the beep...," and recorded, "Emergency. Go to the Coralwood 10 to a movie called *Gangnam, South Korea*. Go to the front row–it's an emergency."

Mom and Dad would hear it, rush to the movies, and I'd get them back together. As crazy as this scheme sounds, I really thought it would work, so I dashed to the theater to see if they both showed up.

After I adjusted to the dark, I located Mom and Dad in the front row arguing with a stranger. "We don't know any Hammer," Mom insisted.

"The message was on my friend's phone," the stranger whined.

Peeking over a chair, I spied a guy with a beak type nose. "Sparrow," I gasped. *He dialed my phone by mistake and figured Hammer left the message*, I thought.

The Mystery of the Glow

The man tried to coax Mom from her seat so he could sit there, but Dad said to leave her alone.

"I'll tell you who he is," I blurted, reaching for Sparrow's wing (opps, I mean arm).

I didn't know it, but Sparrow and I were standing right in front of the movie screen. As the lights from the movie fell on us, we looked like we were *on* the screen and *in* the movie.

The music had a catchy beat.

Sparrow circled me twice, spinning his arm in the air like he had a lasso. I thought he was trying to get me, so I ducked. I twirled a make-believe lasso, so he ducked. I cantered past him.

Moving toward me with both hands out in front, Sparrow had a comical look. I put my hands out in front of me, too, and it looked like we each held a horse rein as our arms pumped up and down and we galloped.

Sparrow put both hands on his hips and looked like he was trotting away. I trotted after him. The audience clapped; a guy called, "Ride 'em, cowboy," and another said, "Mr. Bird is good."

The music was addictive.

Our moves were the same as the actors who were in a dance contest in the movie. On the screen everyone sang "Gangnam Style" as they pumped reins and galloped on invisible horses, but truthfully, Sparrow and I stole the show.

I was confused. Was this a dance?

And the beat went on.

"They're catfish, pretending to be something that they aren't," called out a little lady who was holding a pink cotton candy and pointing at the dancers on the screen. "They're acting high-class like they live in Gangnam, but they don't."

She got up, pumped a make-believe rein, trotted after me, and shoved the candy in my hand. Why? Maybe she thought I won first place in the dance contest.

Sparrow stared at me, and I didn't know what to do, so I jammed the cotton candy at his pointy nose until it stuck. He sneezed and the audience cheered. Boy, they were getting their money's worth. A film *and* a show for a few lousy bucks.

Breathless, Sparrow raced out of the theater, mumbling, "You're nuts! I was just following orders from a friend's phone, and you started dancing."

Some boy called out and told me to dance with the lady. What lady? Glancing up, I saw who he meant— Mom was leaning over me, demanding, "What is the meaning of this?"

"I just wanted you two together," I answered

"Dance yourself right out of here and home, young man," Dad said.

As I raced out, I looked back. That's when I saw the sign that told the audience to get right up and dance along with the movie. And they were. The entire audience was out of control, loudly singing "Gangnam Style" and dancing the invisible horse dance to the catchy beat.

I should have known better than to listen to some dumb underwater creature.

TIME FOR A LAUGH

Outside the bright sunshine punched my eyes as I peeked from behind a newspaper and watched Sparrow scraping the sticky cotton candy off his bright pink face. He dialed a few numbers and told someone to meet him at the mall.

For about an hour, he paced and mumbled. Then a truck zoomed in, the driver sprang out, and he and Sparrow talked. Sparrow told the guy about the movies, but the man wasn't interested. Before long the two of them unloaded all the black and brown plastic bags that were in the man's truck and stacked them in Sparrow's van.

When the van was loaded, the truck sped off, and Sparrow trudged into a store. I decided to tag him. He merely strolled up to the counter and pumped the button that rang for customer assistance.

A clerk who looked like a jolly old elf appeared. He wore scarlet suspenders to hold up his pants because his belt fell below his large, round belly.

The clerk and Sparrow chatted, and Sparrow ordered hundreds and hundreds of labels. He spent a lot of time telling the clerk exactly what to print on the labels. Sparrow kept saying the words "Hammer it home." Every time he said those words, the clerk snapped his suspenders hard and snorted so loud that he made Sparrow laugh.

Sparrow started the order again, and when he got to the "Hammer it home" part, the clerk snapped his suspenders and giggled until his belly shook. All that suspender snapping made Sparrow laugh hysterically. Soon they both bent over and held their sides and hooted until tears came to the clerk's twinkling eyes.

Finally, Sparrow got extra serious—almost angry–and gave exact directions for how to print the labels. I couldn't tell if the whole thing had been business or a joke. Sparrow paid for his order and flew out of there.

Bought the stuff? Boy, was I ever wrong! I thought I'd witness a robbery. To think I had convinced myself he was a crook. Based on what? Wrong phone numbers?

Have you ever doubted yourself? One thing went wrong, and you made mistake after mistake?

It all came into focus. What were the chances Hammer and Sparrow were crooks? That Buck had a grudge? Or that I could get Mom and Dad back together?

My mind was playing tricks on me. I was even starting to take advice from something that lives in the water. I better get ahold of myself.

I laughed right out loud.

CHAPTER FIVE

A Date

Schedules are posted from time to time with new exploratory classes. It was the same old thing. Guidance asked your three top class choices and assigned something else. I had checked marine biology, advance computers, and sports medicine.

I got home economics.

As I entered class, Nicci sat next to a stove, and Buck fooled with a sewing machine on the opposite side of the room. Nicci spoke first, "Great, J. R., you're in this class with me."

For a while Nicci and I yacked about all our classes. Then she mentioned my name. "Does J. R. stand for anything?" she asked.

"Yeah. It's code for handsome," I laughed.

"How silly. I just wondered what it meant."

"Nothing. It means *me*. And what about you?" I wondered.

"Me?"

"Lots of people named Nicci use 'k' as in 'Nikki,'" I said.

"My mom likes unique. Once, I looked it up, and in one language Nicci stands for 'Victory,'" she explained.

"Cool."

"Think you'll like this class, J. R.? Are you a good cook?"

"Yeah, I'm a super chef. Wait 'til you see my pizza," I answered, pretending to toss pizza dough in the air.

"What else have you been cooking up lately?" she asked.

"You wouldn't believe it! Why not come to the yacht club tonight and see. Twinks and I have something you will never believe."

"It's a date. I'll be there," Nicci said as the bell rang to start class.

Nodding, I plopped down and waved a friendly hello to Buck who was staring at me from across the room.

A date, I thought. *She actually said a date. There may be some perks in this class after all. Home ec may just be my favorite class this semester.*

FINDING THE TRUTH

Dancing through the house like a tornado doing the wave to loud music, I got ready to go to the pier.

I can't believe it. I have a date with Nicci.

I looked at my phone messages. One was from Nicci. I smiled and listened. "J. R., sorry, but I can't make it."

Is she playing me for a fool?

RING. I was so busy thinking about Nicci that it startled me when my phone rang; I jumped, and it popped out of my hands. As I picked it back up, I heard Buck's voice. "Look, moron, I tailed you the other day for a reason."

Buck was in the baseball cap? I thought it was Hammer. Why would Buck tail me?

Buck continued, "Stay away from Nicci. Hear me?" He slammed down the phone before I could talk.

It felt like a vampire had sucked my blood.

So that's why Buck chased me all over the river. Because of Nicci! What should I do? No one ever says no to Buck. He always gets everything he wants. And now he wants me.

I lay on my bed, staring at the ceiling. I didn't move a muscle—just stared. I felt like a Pokeman card in Buck's collection.

The Mystery of the Glow

I pictured me and Buck in the boxing ring with a trainer shoving those silly looking gloves at me and a referee who couldn't count to ten.

The phone rang. I stared at it, figuring it was Buck and wondering what to do, broke my trance, and weakly answered, "Hello."

I was surprised: it wasn't Buck; it was Twinks. "J. R., hurry down. R. Mony's here."

"I'll be right down," I said.

Grabbing my diving equipment, I decided my next step. I was going down in the water to see what the mystifying monster was. It was dangerous, but I was going.

For years, deep inside, I had a queasy feeling about swimming. In terror, I had avoided the water at any price. I couldn't even remember why anymore. But it no longer mattered. If I could put up with Nicci saying she wasn't coming over and with Buck bullying me, I could go in the deep and face anything that might be there.

CHAPTER SIX

The Creature Of The Deep

Twinks was so shocked when he saw my diving equipment that he couldn't even pop a knock-knock joke. He stood trembling.

"Not you," he gasped. "You're not diving in that black water."

I knew why. He was remembering what happened when I got my diving certification. We were working on an underwater game, and Twinks wanted to take scuba lessons together even though he knew I hated water. I forced myself through lesson after lesson.

We both passed certification. But the first time we dove together, I got this anxiety attack—like I was being sucked into the bowels of the deep and would drown. Panicking, I grabbed Twinks.

When I rocketed out of the water, Twinks said I rambled and flung my shoes and things into the river.

The Mystery of the Glow

He said that is when he realized that I truly hated the water.

Now, at the yacht club, Twinks was shocked I'd go in again. And in such black water.

He asked, "Why?"

"Things are so bad right now that I have nothing to lose," I answered.

"Wait 'til tomorrow. We'll go together," he begged.

"No. I've got to go now," I said.

"What do you think is down there?"

"Maybe Buck playing a joke," I said. What was down there was the least of my worries. Moving through the water itself would be the hard part, but if I could take all the insults I've had lately, I could do it.

"Don't go," he pleaded.

"Help me with these tanks," I said, slipping the oxygen tank on my back over my wet suit and grabbing a flashlight.

Twinks sprinted to the computer and said, "Let's find out if it will hurt you."

He typed, "Where are you, R. Mony?"

"Here," the mysterious being answered.

Twinks said, "Do you fight?"

"Yes."

Scared for my safety, Twinks quickly typed, "What?"

"Extinction," was the only answer.

"Strange answer," Twinks said.

"You're wasting time. I'm going in." I slipped into the water, sucked on the oxygen tube, and sank into the blackness.

Darkness swallowed me as if I had jumped into a giant bottle of ink. Still and silent ink.

Unable to see my own hand, I switched on the flashlight, forming a circle of light like I had punched a white hole into the ink. All I heard were bubbles and my heart pounding, *anything but water.*

It's scary being here. Why does it have to be so black?

Panic and pain shot through my quivering muscles, and I longed for land. A strange, eerie sensation cut through me as if I had been in these waters before in a disaster. Suffocating.

Why am I doing this?

I continued. Somehow I had no choice. Something pulled me deeper and deeper into the chilly blackness like a lemming heading toward my destiny.

The voice in my head screamed one word over and over. *Danger!*

I swam. My muscles twitched, my scalp tingled with fear, and my pulse quickened. And, to top it all off, my mask was starting to fog.

Within minutes my light blotted out! Extinguished. Like a giant hand had reached out in the darkness and turned it off. I wanted to scream. A smothering feeling filled my soul as if these were my last moments on earth.

Dizziness melted over me.

I had to get out. I knew I had to get out of the water because a panic, deep inside, was starting to grow. Choking me. *I told you never to go in the water again,* the voice in my head said. I raised my hands and pressed them to my ears to stop the voice, but it didn't help.

I knew I had to forget the whole thing and leave, or this would be the end of me.

Then a strange sensation happened. The word *extinction* flashed through my mind. Over and over it pulsed through my being, pulling me like a giant magnet. It was as if the word itself echoed in the murky waters.

Extinction.

Twinks, help me, my brain screamed as I moved on alone, hyperventilating in the black waters.

Then I saw it. My eyes strained as a soft beam beckoned me. Helpless, I followed the blurry, hazy ray of light. I didn't need my flashlight, for on the river's bottom, a fluorescent glow pulsated, lighting the way.

It's hypnotizing me. I had no choice but to propel toward it.

Hanging suspended in the water, I beheld the glow slowly moving toward me.

Closer.

And closer.

Circling me, the creature examined my flippers and squealed in delight.

I was astonished. It looked like a fifteen foot long mermaid. A chunky one with a flat, round body that tapered to a broad, flat tail. It was huge—the size of a small car. And it was fluorescent, glowing in the darkness.

As I hovered and watched the creature, it watched me. As I puzzled over what it was, it puzzled over me. The critter took one of its front paddle-shaped flippers and poked grass into its mouth.

I realized what it was. A MANATEE! One with special powers.

The manatee R. Mony carefully swam closer and rolled over for me to scratch her body, but I couldn't. I was too annoyed. To think I had endangered myself just to find nothing more than this! I had pictured some mysterious, magical being. But she was just a manatee.

An everyday dumb manatee.

How disgusting.

I started to work my way out of the water, feeling silly and betrayed.

THE EXPLANATION

Once I realized there was nothing special down there, my fear of water flooded me again. I surfaced and reached out of the water. A hand gave me a vicious jerk.

It was not Twinks. It was Buck!

I vaguely heard Twinks say, "I got him," as he shoved Buck aside and pulled off my gear.

When Buck got a look at my colorless face, he yelled, "I think he's in shock!"

"We need to help him fast!" Twinks cried.

"What's he got? The bends?" Buck asked.

"It's his reaction from the water," Twinks answered.

Buck did nothing as I flopped up and down like a fish out of water. "He's even weirder than I thought," he grumbled, combing his hair. "Talk about a loser."

"Buck, give me a hand," Twinks said.

"I was down here hanging out at the beach, looking at the girls, and I saw your computer, so I figured I'd find out what you two knuckle heads were up to. But I ain't ever seen anything like this before."

I shook; my face drained. I gagged, doubled over, and tossed my cookies.

"I'm outa here," Buck said as he bolted from the dock. "He might die or something."

"I'm beginning to hate that guy. We don't need him around," Twinks said while rubbing my feet to restore the circulation.

"Me, too. I've had enough for one day," I mumbled.

"Don't worry. J. R., you'll never have to go in the water again."

"I never will," I said emphatically.

When my color returned, Twinks asked, "What was it like down there?"

"The water looked like root beer," I said.

"Did you see anything?"

"Nothing scary. It was a dumb manatee," I shrugged.

Twinks was more impressed than I. "How exciting. A manatee that can communicate with people. What did she look like?"

"Like a spacecraft. A couple thousand pounds with a prehensile upper lip. Had a big Mona Lisa grin, yet reminded me of an elephant," I said. "Had a seal-like body that tapered to a large, flat tail. And something weird."

"Weird?"

"She *glowed*! What could have given her a glow?" I asked.

"That certainly is the biggest mystery of all time," Twinks said.

The Mystery of the Glow

"Come on," I said. "You must know. You always figure out the answers to everything."

"No idea," he answered.

"Something must have happened. Something weird enough to explain why a manatee would glow," I insisted.

"The only weird thing that happened around here lately is the space lab crash 200 miles away," Twinks decided. "They talk about it on the news all the time."

"There wasn't a manatee on it."

"No, there wasn't," he said. Then he got excited. "Wait! There was a CHIP on the space lab. It was being sent to outer space. They went through the Van Allen radiation belts—two regions around Earth with charged particles that have been trapped in the earth's magnetic field."

"So?"

Twinks said that maybe going through the belts made the space lab radioactive, it crashed into the Crystal River, and the CHIP fell out.

"What's that got to do with R. Mony?"

"She was probably at the Crystal River when it crashed," he explained.

Twinks said manatees go to those warm springs during cold snaps because their metabolism is too low to generate heat and their blubber doesn't protect them from cold like dolphins' blubber.

Boy, he's smart.

"They get pneumonia or hypothermia if the water temperature is below 68 degrees," he said. "So they move to warmer water."

"And Mony?" I asked.

"A manatee eats a hundred pounds of vegetation daily. Maybe she ate it and the CHIP's radiation made her special," he said.

"You think?"

"Or maybe it got embedded in her," Twinks decided.

"But how does she communicate with us?" I asked.

"The CHIP has a built in microcomputer and battery, and it emits electrical waves, like radio waves," he said.

"And?"

"Mony's nerve paths act like a big antennae, picking up the waves and transmitting them," Twinks explained.

"Then she came all the way to Cape Coral?" I asked

"Yup. They can travel 50 miles in one day."

"And?"

"It was Mony that Buck's boat hit. Manatees go to the power plant for the same reason—to stay warm in the water discharge," Twinks said.

"Amazing. But I'm not interested in manatees."

"J. R., you're kidding. The greatest find ever, and you don't care because she's a sea cow?'

Shrugging, I stomped away.

"J. R., you are, without a doubt, the most stubborn person I know!"

CHAPTER SEVEN

Mony's Essence

Mrs. Peach had taught home economics so long she looked like a home ec project. Her pink and purple floral printed dress fell to neat folds like an ironed tablecloth, and she used lemon soap and apple scented perfume. When she got near, it smelled like a basket of fruit had just walked by. Her long, blonde hair had white tips and when piled high in waves, it looked like her head was a giant lemon meringue pie.

She had the class submit projects that we wanted to do and posted the names on the class bulletin board. I slinked over to peek at the list. Kids could do whatever they wanted, and the list went on and on forever.

Ed J. wanted to circulate a banner around the whole school to welcome home military vets, Sharon and Vincent were cooking the Italian Feast of the Seven Fishes, Maggie was featuring a gluten free dessert with wild berries that she grew herself, and Mike and Bailey were going to demonstrate campfire grilling of wild boar in the wilderness.

But where was my name?

I realized Mrs. Peach had posted two lists on the wall. I moseyed over to the second one.

Deb had signed up to Feng shui the principal's office, Emily wanted to bake, and Nicci picked sewing. Of all the crazy things, Buck's project was hair designs. Buck and friends were already in the back of the room with electric razors, cutting and dyeing each other's hair.

My name was at the bottom under cooking. I picked cooking because it would be an easy "A." How hard can it be to make Jell-O? Any fool could do it.

But not me.

The directions said to pour the powdery, cherry contents of the box into a bowl and add one cup of hot water and one of cold. The problem was that I had used two boxes and didn't double the water amount; I was too distracted watching all the different projects around the room.

When I sniffed apples, I knew I was sunk. Mrs. Peach was next to me and she didn't have that "you're about to get an *A*" look in her eye. She carefully explained that I had doubled the Jell-O but hadn't doubled the water, so I had the wrong measurements, and it would become a huge, rubbery blob.

What great news for me. I may have stumbled onto something new that we can use in our inventions. Maybe we'll invent a red, rubbery soccer ball. *Wait 'til I tell Twinks,* I thought.

"Want a trim?" Buck asked me half-jokingly as he strolled around the room combing his hair.

Ignoring him, I took out a box of pancake mix and started whistling and stirring until Buck passed my area again and nudged me aside.

"Put that entire huge pancake in one pan, and I'll get you a shovel to flip it," Buck clowned as he handed me the largest fry pan in the class. I could see by his expression that he planned on forcing me to make a pancake bigger than a table.

I continued stirring. Buck was being Buck because that's his whole show, and that wasn't going to end well for me.

He firmly took my hand to stop me from cooking and said, "Look at Emily over there. She's making a dump cake. See how she does it? She just dumps the mix into a bowl and then dumps the fruit in. Why don't you make one, too? And when you're done, what do you think I could do with it?"

I slipped my hand loose.

Buck hummed, "Dump-de-dump dump."

I moved back from him and added blueberries to my pancake mix.

Buck combed his hair back and said, "Hey, meathead, want to putt-putt up to Sun Splash Waterpark with us today? You know—slides and water. It will be even better than the boat shower and the scuba dive put together." He smirked.

I was glad Nicci was absent so she didn't see him bully me. What could she have in common with someone like Buck?

"Ain't I bad?" Buck sneered as he slipped away from my area to the back of the room.

The sounds of clicking scissors, buzzing razors, and whirling hair dryers filled the room like a giant beehive. Hair snips blanketed the tile floor. Mrs. Peach sidled up to Buck and told him not to get carried away. Buck shrugged his shoulders, put on his most innocent expression, flashed a huge Cheshire cat grin, and told her that he didn't do it.

"I didn't do it," one of his friends imitated Buck.

"It's not my fault. Duh," Buck added.

"I didn't do it. We didn't mean it," the group echoed.

"Get back to work," Mrs. Peach announced with a raised eyebrow.

At the end of class, when I looked back there, I saw some boys with new haircuts. One letter of the alphabet was shaved like a brand in the back of each knobby head. Others had used dye on their hair, and their heads looked like round Easter eggs with brightly colored letters in the center.

They stood in a line and the letters formed a sentence. To anyone looking, they spelled out, "I DIDN'T DO IT."

YIN-YANG

Friday, Nicci was back in school, and she entered home ec with a jacket tossed over her arm. "What silly haircuts," she giggled.

"You know Buck's friends," I answered softly.

"I notice Buck doesn't have a letter on his head," she added.

"But he got those kids to do it," I said.

"Exactly my point," she said and turned to sew her jacket sleeve. I walked away from Nicci like Buck had warned me.

At the end of class, she was done sewing and put the jacket on. I flew out of my cubicle. "What's that design on your jacket?" I demanded in astonishment. It was the same symbol Mony had sent us.

"It's a mandala of yin-yang. It's an ancient symbol that basically means that nothing is all black or all white. It represents balance. I got this jacket at tai chi before the accident. It means harmony," Nicci answered.

"Harmony! That's what Mony wanted to tell us when we met, but she couldn't think of the word. I said we were 'man' and she wanted to say 'ha<u>rmony</u>' but was having trouble explaining, so she sent up a picture. A mandala of yin-yang. Then she figured how to spell it, but we only understood the last part—RMONY!" I said.

I quickly filled Nicci in about our encounter with a manatee named R. Mony, and how I now understood what her name meant. Nicci asked me to explain more.

"I've no idea. I'm personally not in harmony," I growled.

"Maybe someday, J. R."

"Never."

"I love manatees," she said. "That's why I want to be a marine biologist to protect them from red tide. Red tide killed 267 manatees in Southwest Florida last year."

"I'm not…"

Nicci interrupted me. "Red tide affects their nervous system, and they can drown unless we help them. There's even a free iPhone app people can use to report a harmed manatee."

"I'm not interested in them or the water," I whined.

"Maybe that's your problem. You are *out* of harmony. Maybe that's why R. Mony came here of all places!"

We were so busy talking that I didn't notice Buck, fuming with anger, standing behind Nicci. He pointed at the backs of the heads of all his friends who had lined up in such a way that the letters cut and dyed on the back of each head spelled out words. I gulped as I read the message referring to me talking to Nicci.

"DON'T DO IT!!!"

I breathed a sigh of relief as the bell rang.

HYACINTHS

The next few days were a nightmare. Everywhere I went, Buck and friends were flashing words from the backs of their heads. Twinks said he heard Buck wanted all the kids at school to cut or color words in their hair so it would look like they were all sending messages to me. I was so not impressed that I wished I would wake up and the whole crummy thing would go away.

All of the Cyclones were at Pelican Field. I told Twinks I just didn't want to see anybody, skipped our practice, and biked to Trafalgar Field, so I could be alone. For the first hour, I sprinted until I was ready to drop.

Next, I just juggled, trying to see how long I could keep the ball from hitting the ground without using my hands. No time to think of the mess I was in—just me and the ball. Thump. Thump. One lapse of focus, and I'd lose my rhythm and drop it. I juggled for an hour straight.

I started to feel human again.

Soon I heard the text alert on my phone, and Twinks texted me to come to his house to hide. I wasn't interested, but we typed awhile, and he talked me into it.

When I got there, I was shocked that he wasn't alone; Nicci and R. Mony were there, too. Twinks had coaxed the unusual manatee there with the water hyacinth plants that grew along his canal.

By the time I arrived, things were in full swing. Nicci was communicating with Mony, and I got the surprise of my life. Nicci was *talking into the system.*

"Is this one of your jokes, Twinks?"

"Did you hear me say knock-knock?" he said sarcastically.

"Very funny," I moaned. "Is Nicci actually talking into the system? How can that be?" I asked.

"It's all based on how I tie into the miniature microcomputer from the CHIP," Twinks answered. "Just like when we talk into an iPad."

(I *told* you he was smart!!!!)

"This sure is one high powered set up," I said.

"It will win the science fair," he answered.

Sitting nearby, I watched Nicci talk into the computer as R. Mony answered while munching some flowering plants. I heard the plants crunching as I leaned over Nicci's shoulder to see what the two of them were up to.

"You love those flowers, don't you?" Nicci said into the system.

"All manatees love them." Mony's impulses moved through the water like sound waves and floated across the monitor as words.

"Delicate. Right, R. Mony?" Nicci said.

"I love Delicates!" Mony answered, rolling over.

Nicci turned toward me and explained that the water hyacinth is one of a manatee's favorite plants to eat.

"Somehow Mony thinks hyacinths are called 'Delicates'," Nicci said, laughing. "Isn't that adorable?"

I mumbled that the whole thing was silly, and Nicci said to lighten up. I probably would have relaxed and enjoyed the day if I had known what was going to happen to me the next day.

CHAPTER EIGHT

Somebody Better Take Action

The next day started sunny. I was surprised when my doorbell rang. Surprised because no one ever used it. Surprised Twinks didn't say to "ants her"(answer) the door.

And surprised when I answered; it was Nicci.

"I couldn't get Mony off my mind," she said.

"Oh, I thought it was me you wanted to see," I joked. "Come in. Twinks and I are heating up leftover pizza from Papa Joe's and working on our school project. Did you do yours yet?"

"Yes. I adopted a manatee from the Save the Manatee Club," she said.

"We're doing 'owl gebra'," Twinks laughed. "Our report is burrowing owls."

"Awesome. Cape's official bird. We have the largest population of Florida burrowing owls in the world,"

Nicci said. "They're so rad. Wouldn't it be cool if you could turn your head 270 degrees like they can?"

I turned my head to see how many degrees it turns.

"It's fun watching them extend their home by kicking dirt so fast that it flies out like a dust storm," she said. "And you should find out why they 'decorate' their burrow entrance with shiny objects and bits of trash."

"They're a 'hoot'," Twinks said.

"Cape Coral *is* a Burrowing Owl—unique and needs to be protected," Nicci said.

Twinks heated a slice of tasty pizza until it was steamy and spooned her some Papa Joe's salad flecked with cold cuts and cheese. Hearing the crunch and seeing the gooey cheese stretch when Nicci took a bite made my mouth water, even though I just finished all of mine.

Nicci found it hard to eat hot pizza and laugh at the same time, but she did as Twinks popped out joke after joke. Then he told her how Mony got the CHIP and about our day on the boat with Buck.

"Do you think Buck's boat hit Mony?" she asked.

"Yup. Buck was speeding all over—not caring about speed zones or what was in the water, and he plowed into her," Twinks said.

"That's awful."

The Mystery of the Glow

"It would have hurt any regular manatee, but Mony has special powers and survived it," Twinks explained. "Boats kill about a hundred manatees in Florida every year."

As he and Nicci talked, I checked my phone. My only message was from Sparrow. "Hammer? This is Sparrow. Just making sure nothing's changed, and that we're keeping our plan to meet at the marina tomorrow night at 8:00. I have what we need. We'll soon be rich!"

"Nicci! Twinks!" I shouted. "Wait 'til you hear the message on my phone! I told you they were up to no good."

After they listened, I could tell by looking at Twinks that he thought Hammer and Sparrow were up to something bad. "Listen to his tone of voice!" Twinks exclaimed. "You were right all along, J.R."

"Come on, you two," Nicci calmly said. "You're reading too much into this."

I played the message again.

Nicci's eyes opened wider and wider. Her body language changed, her voice got tense, and she firmly said, "Let's go and see what they are up to."

WAITING

The following day we got to the yacht club at 6:00 p. m., went to the picnic tables by the pool, and ate the food Nicci brought from Nelly's Greek restaurant.

"Opa!" Nicci exclaimed. "Want a gyro, J. R.?"

"What is it?" I wondered.

"They roast a huge hunk of meat on a giant spit and shave it to order right in front of you," Nicci explained.

I took a couple bites of the sandwich. "Wow. It's yummy," I said.

When I had trouble pronouncing "gyro," Nicci said, "Think of a calendar: days, weeks, months, and 'year-o'."

We spied on the nearby marina while chomping on the gyros and hummus.

By 7:00, we had chowed down and hidden behind a boat near the tennis court section of the yacht basin. As we scanned the area for Hammer, Twinks said, "It feels like we're three characters in a mystery."

"Let's hope it has a happy ending," I answered.

After a few minutes, Twinks said, "I'm gonna make like a tree and leave," and strolled over to case the area where the boats refuel. Nicci and I stayed behind on lookout.

"Tell me if you see anything dangerous," I told Nicci, who was staring through binoculars.

As she looked up and down the basin at the boats anchored at the marina, I watched some divers clean their equipment, hosing it down while chatting about scuba diving the USS Mohawk off Sanibel. When they were done, row after row of neon pink and turquoise masks and flippers were lined up on boxes to dry.

Finally, Nicci turned my way and zeroed in on me through the binoculars.

"You know what, J. R.?" Nicci said.

"What?"

"You're kind-a-cute."

She took me completely off guard. I felt my face heat up.

"Especially when you blush," she added.

At 7:30, Twinks raced toward us and slid into our hiding place behind the boat like a baseball player sliding into home plate. "Shhhh," he whispered. "Here comes a boat."

"Sparrow!" Nicci exclaimed, pointing at a man with a nose that looked like a bird's beak. It was the same man who danced with me at the movies.

Sparrow docked. Men unloaded boxes, piled them on the wharf, and carried them to some of the other boats that were tied up at the marina. Gosh, there were lots of boxes. Why did they need all that stuff?

At 8:00 sharp, a tough looking man joined Sparrow. His squared off head had a wide forehead, and two shifty eyes bulged on the sides of it. They were spread so far apart that they appeared to be on his temples. "Hammer!" I gasped.

"That's him. Even looks like a hammerhead shark," Nicci murmured.

Hammer blasted Sparrow a few times and barked out orders for everyone to hurry. But Hammer did no manual labor.

IT STINKS

The men took forever to finish unloading Sparrow's boat. It seemed twice as long for us because we couldn't stand the smell.

We stayed hidden until they finished. The three of us froze in position until they were out of our sight for a long, long time. When we were sure they were gone and it was safe, we spoke. Twinks was first. "Knock. Knock."

"Who's there?"

"Jester."

"Jester who?" Nicci said, giggling.

"Jester minute more and we can finally get out of this smelly area," Twinks said.

"Phew!"

"What stinks?" I asked.

As usual, Twinks knew; he pointed to the purple and red algal blooms.

"Algae smell bad?" I gagged. "Crummy. What caused them to be here?"

Twinks said it was from Lake Okeechobee releasing water down the Caloosahatchee River, causing algae to grow.

"Was that what made the water black when I met Mony?" I asked.

"Yup, the released water is dirty because of farm runoff," Twinks answered.

"Someone has to stop Lake O from polluting the Caloosahatchee River," I said.

"There's also the problem of our own local runoff feeding the algae," Twinks said.

"I saw that on TV the other day," Nicci said. "They said not to fertilize during rainy season; the runoff from nitrogen and phosphorus hurts our waterways."

"Someone needs to figure this out," I said.

Nicci was mad. "Someone needs to save our beautiful waterways."

"Our real estate and jobs, "Twinks added.

"Our tourism," Nicci said. "Our economy's based on clean water."

We held our noses.

"Somebody needs to put a wrench in the stench," Twinks said. Guess what he did next?

"Knock. Knock."

"Who's there?" Nicci asked.

"Lettuce."

"Lettuce who?" Nicci giggled.

The Mystery of the Glow

"Lettuce close class for the day," Twinks said. He hesitated and added, "We need to check out these guys. I'm going to make like a hat and go on ahead."

Twinks signaled me to call the cops and slipped out of sight.

CHAPTER NINE

Heart To Heart

"Call Buck," Nicci calmly said. "Instead of the cops? Why?"

"We don't even know if there is anything illegal going on, and he lives near here," she explained.

I pulled out my cell phone and dialed Buck's number.

"Yeah?" he answered on the first ring. I could hardly hear him over the pounding music he was playing. Whispering, I told our plight.

"Who? Speak up or hang up," he demanded.

I repeated the message, explaining we were at the yacht basin, and it was swarming with bad guys.

"I'm near the marina. I could find you," Buck bragged.

I puffed a sigh of relief and muttered, "Call the cops and tell them."

"Sure. The fuzz should know."

"Thanks, Buck. I owe you!"

"You do, but I won't be there to collect. Sucker!"

"Help us."

"I was just gonna take a nap," Buck yawned.

"Help Nicci; she's here," I begged.

"Hey, if she's nuts enough to hang with you, she gets what she deserves."

"Nobody's that mean," I said as he slammed down the phone.

GETTING TO KNOW NICCI

Nicci was furious. I never saw those veins on her neck pop like that before.

"Nicci, you can't save all the jerks in the world. Forget him," I said.

"It's not just Buck," she said. "I'm angry about the algae. I'm used to sparkling waters that look like someone brushed them with gold dust. Used to pelicans and fish and gentle manatees. I don't want anything to ruin all of that."

Nicci explained that when there's lots of rain, Lake O releases water so their aging dike doesn't leak. "That upsets the delicate balance of *our* water," she said.

She sure loves Southwest Florida, I thought.

"People need to realize that even paradise is fleeting if they don't guard it," she said.

Nicci once read that upstream from the Fort Myers Bridge there used to be thick grass—like a lush meadow for manatees—but not anymore.

She said, "The Caloosahatchee is an estuary and needs the right mix of salt and fresh water. Algae smother our sea grasses when too much fresh water is released, *and* when too little is let go, our water gets too salty."

Either way we lose our sea grasses.

"Manatees are herbivores and depend on the grasses to live," she said. "Poor Mony and her friends."

"Look, Nicci, I'm not crazy about all this water stuff."

"What about Mony?"

"Me, take ideas from a sea cow? I don't think so," I huffed.

"But, J. R., her harmony ideas! Look at us. People can't get along. Wars. Pollution. The world's a mess. It's obvious to our generation. Mony is giving us the message to seek a balance."

"We do have a mess," I agreed. "Look at Hammer. Look at Buck."

"Buck has problems," she said.

"Buck *is* a problem. Why does he act that way?" I asked.

"His parents never said no and he started running things. He manipulates them, and they back him up," Nicci explained.

"He's starting to believe his own act. He's a bully!"

"He's on the wrong track now, but Buck once had a soft spot," Nicci said.

"His only soft spot is between the ears."

"He was O.K. last year; that's why I hung out with him," she explained.

"You did?" I was amazed.

"Yes," she said.

"Some kids said that, but I thought it was a rumor," I said.

"They weren't sure. Mom knew."

"Your mom? How'd she find out?" I asked.

"The day of the accident."

"Accident," I gasped. "You were with Buck?"

"Yeah. He talked me into riding an ATV with him on some empty lots. It started to rain and got slippery. I begged him to quit. But impulsive Buck got some kid to race him. Before I knew it…," Nicci shuddered.

I wished I could say something to shield her from such a terrible memory.

She continued, "Wind in my hair. Rain pounding my eyes. The skids. The screams."

"Wow," I said sadly.

"We were both thrown out of the ATV, but Buck was lucky. Just scrapes and bruises. Hardly anything."

"You?"

"I lay there in pain as they scattered. Left me there," she shuddered.

"Left you?" I asked, barely able to believe what I was hearing.

"Scared of the police," Nicci said.

"I can't believe Buck would do such a rotten thing," I said.

The Mystery of the Glow

"Slowly, painfully, I dragged myself toward the main road and lay there an hour or so, unable to move. I pushed and pulled. Finally, an ambulance came with Mom. Buck had phoned her when he realized he couldn't just leave me there," she said.

"And he never told anyone?" I asked.

"No. Me neither until now."

"I'm so sorry, Nicci."

"Mom was great," she continued. "Never yelled about the whole thing. Saw me every day at the hospital. Slowly, I realized why she has rules. She's awesome. My best friend. A year of treatments, and she was always there. Buck never called once."

And he has the nerve to poke his nose in my business to tell me to stay away from her. "The jerk," I said.

"Kids take on roles. After a while the role sticks. That's what happened to him."

"You've given it a lot of thought, Nicci."

"A year in therapy. Lots of time to think."

"What do you think of him now?" I asked.

"He's O.K.; I've had to put him straight a few times. Like after he said he'd ruin my victory party if you came," Nicci said.

That explains it all. Why she stayed clear of me. Why Buck followed and phoned and threatened me.

"Well, you certainly figured out one thing in all this harmony jazz, Nicci."

"What?" she asked.

"How to be in harmony with yourself. Maybe that is the best harmony of all."

OPENING OLD WOUNDS

"What about you, J. R.?"

"Me?"

"You seem troubled. What is it?" Nicci asked.

"Troubled? You got to be kidding," I said.

"What's the worst thing that ever happened to you?" she asked.

"Aside from Hammer and Buck?" I answered.

"Other than them."

"My parents' divorce makes me feel rotten," I said.

"Why?"

"Can't we talk about something else?" I moaned.

"Sure. How about Mony," Nicci suggested.

"Nicci, you've got a way of talking about topics I'm not into."

"Why?"

"I don't even know." I said. "My mom loves the environment. You'd think it would be important to me, but it's not. It brings a feeling of panic."

"Something caused this. Think. Can't you remember why, J. R.?"

Sparrow and a couple guys came back and climbed aboard Sparrow's boat. "Shhhh," I warned her. "They will catch us."

We sat quietly, side to side. I leaned back and started thinking. Thinking about something that happened five years before.

My mind faded back to that day. Suddenly, after all these years, I could see it. Sun drenched beaches and laughter and diving in search of underwater critters. It had been a perfect day with Mom.

And then she told me. That it was over. She loved me but had to go—it wasn't working between her and Dad, and she had things she had to do.

Like what? I cried. What's so important? Sea life, she answered. She explained that they were divorcing. She'd live nearby but would travel a lot with an environmental group to save green sea turtles.

"Save green sea turtles? Who cares about dumb sea life?" I cried. "What about *our lives?*"

Mom hugged me, but I just got more hysterical. "I hate you both. And if I caused the divorce, I'm glad," I cried, jumping into the water. My legs tangled in some nearby ropes and diving weights that yanked me to the bottom. Struggling and gasping, I tried to free myself.

There was a haze.

Then nothing.

When I came to, I was in the hospital with them by my side. I got better. And Mom left.

For a year, I biked to the beach and cursed the water and threw rocks at it. I vowed to never go near the water again. Since then I felt empty—as if I were still drowning.

And here I was years later, still wishing they'd get back together. Still feeling guilty for something and not even knowing what it was. Still hating the sea and even Mony.

I sat shaking, sweating, and breathing heavily. And for the first time in my life, I understood my panic. My fears.

Understood myself.

My thoughts were interrupted by a Twinks' whistle that sounded like a bird in the distance. It was the secret whistle we created in kindergarten.

When Twinks arrived, he uttered that he had seen a few mighty suspicious things going on. I whispered that Sparrow had returned from the other boats and was close by, down in the cabin of his own.

Even with that nearby threat, Twinks was able to squeeze out a joke.

"Knock. Knock."

"Who's there?" Nicci mouthed.

"Ima," Twinks said quietly.

"Ima who?"

"Ima sorry to tell you, but J. R. was right all along. Hammer and Sparrow are criminals," Twinks muttered.

"We got to get out of here fast," I whispered as we sneaked away.

Moving along was creepy because I knew that any minute someone might hear us, and we'd get captured. My hands sweated, and every noise made me flinch or duck into the shadows.

As we passed Sparrow's boat, I was afraid Nicci was scared until she grinned and made motions like she was a little sparrow flying away. Her eyes twinkled as she twittered, and she was beaming as she said in a hushed voice, "Knock. Knock."

"Who's there?" Twinks murmured.

"Safari."

"Safari who?" Twinks asked.

"Safari so good," Nicci sighed as we melted into the night.

THE REUNION

When we looked back at Sparrow's boat, he was still inside, and we could see papers scattered all around and money being passed out.

Without uttering a word, we moved in the darkness. I left Nicci and Twinks by the fountain, slinked along the edge of the beach, and scanned the river for Mony. As I stood there looking, a cold, clammy object dropped firmly on my shoulder and clutched it. "Going somewhere?" a rough voice asked.

I gulped.

"What are you kids up to?" the voice snarled.

I looked over my other shoulder and found myself closer to the water than I'd ever want to be.

"Going somewhere, Putt-Putt?"

I held my breath. Not many people used that name for me. "Buck!" I gasped, turning completely around and peering into his icy eyes. "What are you doing here?"

"Looks like a dang school reunion, doesn't it?" Buck growled.

"Help us before it's too late; I'll never tell," I said.

"Never tell? You already did when you called and told me about these guys. At first I thought you were your everyday weird self, like putting computers in the water, but then I realized this news would make me rich," Buck boasted, puffing up his chest and scraping his fingers through his hair.

I tried to step past him, but he blocked me.

His massive body was a barrier, and the only way past was to step in the water. As I did, he splashed water at my face, squarely jammed his shoulder against mine, and laughed wildly.

In a flash I decided not to put up with this any longer; it was time to stand up to him. Using every ounce of my body, I tightened up, ignored the water, and focused directly on Buck. Pulling my shoulders back, I stood straight, and tried to stare him down, eyeball to eyeball.

This would be our final showdown. No matter what happened, Buck would finally realize I wouldn't put up with him any longer. I was sure if I stood firm, he'd back down.

Without so much as a blink, I shuffled toward him. He was stunned. Unsure of what to do next. Just as I expected. Some people are not so brave when they don't have a bunch of guys standing behind them.

But I'll never know because as I inched toward him, I stepped in a hole, lost my balance, and plunged into the river, sucking in such a huge mouthful of water that my lungs were ready to explode. I began to panic.

The Mystery of the Glow

A silent yet hysterical panic.

Not water. Not again.

A gray haze filled my head.

I'm drowning, I thought. Dizzy and limp, I collapsed and crumbled to the bottom.

Twinks jumped in. Luckily, he had come to see what took me so long. He flipped me over and pumped my aching lungs until water squirted out like the fountain at school.

"Get away, Twinks," Buck sneered. "This has nothing to do with you." Buck shoved Twinks away so hard that he tumbled and scraped his face on the pier, causing his chin to split open and his eye to squirt blood.

When Twinks wiped away the blood, he was face to face with Hammer. "Enough," Hammer snarled in anger.

"Get their phones. Then find the girl and lock her and Twinks up in that old boathouse and nail the door shut," he ordered Buck. "It has no windows and hangs over the water, so there's no way to escape."

As Buck and Twinks trudged away, I heard Twinks courageously spit out a "Knock. Knock."

"Cut it out," Buck grumbled.

"No more joking around," Hammer said.

"What about him?" Buck pointed to me.

"He's almost unconscious, so I'll tie him to a piling. When you've locked up the other two, come back for him," Hammer snarled.

"Good enough," Buck said, combing and puffing and patting his hair.

Hammer smiled at Buck and boasted, "You know, kid, when you came to tell me you knew about J. R., I wasn't sure I trusted you, but you've paid off. There's a place in my organization for you."

Buck flexed his muscles and grinned.

Hammer grabbed me under my arm pits, dragged me to a piling, and tied me to it.

As Buck herded up Twinks and Nicci, he called back, "What will we do with them?"

"There's a firework barge off shore. They'll get blamed for setting it off," Hammer huffed.

Just what we need, I thought. *To be fireworks in a 4th of July display.*

My weary head crashed to the deck and I passed out.

Chapter 10: The Mystery of the Glow

MONY'S MAGIC

With the three of us captured, it fell to one being alone to stop Hammer.

R. Mony.

But what could a lone manatee do?

She had powers beyond human imagination. Mony lay off the lighted wharf in deep water, submerged, taking in information. It had been easier when we used the computer. Getting vibrations from life itself took extra concentration.

What could she do? No impulses. No ideas came. All that came to her being, pulsating around her in the murky waters, were images of us captured.

Visions of love.

The 2,000 pound sea cow lay depressed on the muddy river bottom.

Sad. Lonely. Hopeless.

R. Mony wished animals had a strong kinship with people. But they were separated into different kingdoms. People didn't believe enough for her to contact them. She'd have to figure it out for herself.

She lay still. Heart-broken.

Suddenly, the fluorescent glow brightened. It started pulsating like when a light switch turns on and off. The mud stirred. The surrounding water started to slowly ripple as the beam pulsed stronger.

THE UNEXPECTED

Cold water splashed in my eyes. "Cut it out," I moaned as it dripped through my hair and down my face until I tasted salt water.

Where am I? Dizzy, I tried to stand but couldn't.

I peeked through stinging eyes at my hands tied to a piling. *Someone tied me with a slipknot. Where are Twinks and Nicci?* I thought.

I couldn't think, but I knew this was an epic fail. My head pounded, and my injured arm was stretched out and tied. I felt like a soda without the fizz. Deeper and deeper I plunged into the purple haze.

Plop! Water sprayed, waking me up. "Who's there?" I coughed.

My only answer was a thump in the water. Stretching, I spied a coconut shaped glow popping out of the river.

"Mony!" I exclaimed.

She edged closer to the dock and nuzzled my nose. "How did you know?" I asked.

Her whiskers tickled my forehead. I saw her beady eyes and felt her trunk-like, wet nose. The smell of the sea stuck to her chin. "Mony, I can't believe it; I'm actually glad to see you."

Mony made a squeaking sound.

"I don't know how you found us, but if you knew this, you know these men are dangerous. We got to get out of here fast," I told her.

R. Mony mouthed the rope. Fortunately, a slip knot is easy to undo, and slowly, the slip knot loosened until it untied. I struggled to stand, but she motioned at the water.

"Water? Are you kidding?" I laughed.

She gestured again. I scanned the water, wondering what to do. As I did, the strangest feeling flooded my being and washed the panic from my soul.

Slowly, I slipped in. I shook violently from the chilly waters—but not from fear.

Not from fright!!!

Could facing my fear and knowing why I was petrified have made such a difference? I dove under and resurfaced laughing. I had done it. I had conquered my anxieties!

"I'm free!" I exclaimed.

Mony squealed with joy and rolled over and over.

For a few minutes I reveled in my glory. "This is me, J. R., happy in the water!" I said.

Tickled.

At peace.

The Mystery of the Glow

"This is a cool idea, Mony. They'd catch me on land but not in the water," I said as she signaled me to follow.

Swimming closely behind, I was amazed that I had no horrifying fear of the water. I was even more astonished that I had such trust in a sea cow!

She steered with her flippers, and her body and tail undulated, moving her along with a wavelike motion. Since manatees can go 20 miles per hour, I was glad she was only traveling two or three; she was going easy on me, and I did my best to keep up.

We were a parade.

I stopped to wipe the water from my eyes and watched her surface every couple minutes for a breath. Then she plunged out of sight.

"Pssssst, Mony, where are you?" As I spoke, I tasted the salt water, and it didn't bring dread. It just made me think of pretzels.

Treading water to stay in place, I looked all around me, but she was gone. Manatees can submerge for 20 minutes, and I couldn't just hang in one spot waiting. I was relieved when a glowing coconut popped out of the water. When she surfaced, I heard a rushing sound as she exhaled forcefully through her nostrils.

"I'm happy to see you, Mony," I said and joined her.

I was glad she glowed. It was a beacon in the darkness.

It helped me follow; when I opened my eyes under water, I could distinguish her, looking like a giant balloon in the darkness. In the shallow areas, her stout, nailed flippers moved her along the bottom. In the murky water, Mony propelled her tail up and down and used the hairs on her body to get information about currents and objects in the water.

We moved together in the night.

Swosh.

Smack.

All I heard was an occasional swoosh sound from Mony's breathing and the slap of her tail. We swam side by side in the chilly water with me thinking, *We are swimming together. I never thought it would happen to me.*

NO WAY OUT

By the time we surfaced, I was so out of breath that I was a windmill without a breeze. Glancing up, I realized I was past the tennis courts and on the far side of the yacht basin near the old boathouse that was being torn down to extend parking. The building had no windows, and the door was all nailed up.

Treading water, I looked for R. Mony. I saw no glow. No manatee. She had disappeared again. "Pssssst," I whispered. "Mony, where are you?"

She popped through the water's surface.

"Boy, am I glad to see you. Stay with me. Stop playing games. I'm getting out of breath," I said, huffing and puffing.

She firmly nudged me and stared directly in my eyes. I could tell this was not a game. *Whatever she's trying to tell me is important,* I thought.

Mony submerged and slapped her tail on the boards above her. She was beneath the shabby boathouse.

"Do you think Twinks might be in there?" I asked excitedly.

She rolled over and over in the water and squealed with joy as she motioned with her flipper.

"How can we help him?"

Mony partially submerged, and as she did, her tail flipped against the bottom of the sagging structure.

THUMP.

She did it again.

THUMP.

I reached up and knocked, but nothing happened. Now what? This wasn't working; I was out of breath and my knuckles were bruised from all the pounding.

Scratch!

Scratch!

Directly above me, a scraping sound echoed in the night. Rats? The thought of being greeted by rats gnawed at my mind, making me quiver with fright, but I punched the boards until my arms ached.

Grabbing a piling to hold onto, I heard it–someone knocking back. "I hope it's Twinks," I said. Frantic hammering noises intensified until a board loosened and slid aside. Debris and grit tumbled into my eyes.

"Way to go, Mony. It's open," I cheered. Reaching through the opening, I felt someone's hand slowly touch my fingertips, clutch my wrist, and give a tremendous yank. Flying into the room like I was diving *out* of the water, I hoped it wasn't Hammer grabbing my arm.

It wasn't. It was Twinks and Nicci. Even though I couldn't see them in the blackness of the old boathouse,

The Mystery of the Glow

I knew. Choking from all of the dank, musty mildew that stole my voice, at first I couldn't mutter a word. Finally, I coughed in relief, "It's really you! Am I glad it's you two!"

"J. R., you came by water, no less! Cool!" Twinks said.

Nicci spoke, "How did you find us?"

"Easy. I had a guide." I pointed to the hole in the floor. Mony popped through the opening, and her soft glow filled the room.

"Mony!" Nicci exclaimed, as she huddled next to Twinks on the dirty floor.

"Now I've seen everything," Twinks gasped. "J. R. traveling with a manatee."

"You're no more surprised than I am," I said. "She'll save you next."

We three gave the high five. Then I saw it. "Twinks, are you all right?"

"It's nothing–just Buck's calling card," he said.

"There's a gouge near your eye."

"I got it at Buck's reunion," he laughed. Dried blood caked the side of his face. Quickly, I took off my shirt and started ripping it into strips. I gently wrapped it round and round Twinks' head. The white bandage circled his black face with love.

Then I spoke. "Twinks, go first."

Without hesitation, he slipped in the water, holding the bandage securely against his head and saying, "Knock. Knock."

"Who's there?" Nicci and I asked.

"Gouda."

"Gouda who?" Nicci asked.

"Gouda go. Pretty cheesy joke. Right?" he said.

We laughed.

Twinks grinned and added, "I'm going to make like an atom and split," and he disappeared into the water.

Minutes later, Mony's glow filtered back into the dingy room as she returned for Nicci. I told Nicci to go for it and that Mony had signaled for her to hold on.

As Nicci lowered herself into the water, I pictured how frightened she probably was.

"J. R., what about you?" she asked.

"I'll be O.K."

"Hammer could be here any minute," she warned.

"I'm going to hide in the water after I slip those floor boards back in place, so they'll never guess where you two went," I said.

Nicci giggled.

"It's time for a victory," I kidded.

She snickered and raised her two fingers in a "V" for victory.

"Now, hurry," I commanded.

"Don't worry; I'll be O.K.," she said.

"Just take a deep breath, Nicci, and trust in Mony."

"There is something I must tell you," Nicci said.

"Hurry. Tell me," I said.

I figured she had some fears to get off her chest, so I might as well let her.

"J. R., you sure look cute when you're wet," she said as she winked and plunged out of sight.

Within minutes, Mony returned for me. When we surfaced, I clutched the edge of the sea wall and scurried like a crab along the slippery deck to where my friends were hiding.

We looked at each other and laughed.

Twinks asked, "Aren't you afraid of water anymore?"

"Not," I answered.

"What was your aha moment?" Nici asked.

"YOLO. Lots to tell, but she wants me to hurry," I said.

"J. R., you're starting to scare me," Twinks said. "Talking to a manatee like you're doing."

"I never thought I'd be bonding with one," I answered.

Mony was getting impatient.

"We got to get moving," I said. "Mony will help you two out to that barge. Untie it and wait for our signal."

"How is she able to help us like this?" Nicci asked.

"She has special powers, but even regular manatees *are* smarter than people think," Twinks said.

"Hurry," I urged.

"O.K., I'll do whatever Mony says since she saved us once already," Twinks said. "Maybe she does have a plan or two up her sleev…"

"Up her flipper," I interrupted him. "Hurry, I'll wait here for Mony to come back."

"It's hard to believe. First, you at home in the water, and then you and nature as one," Twinks told me as they slipped away.

"Nothing to it," Nicci said. "J. R. is finally in harmony with himself, and when you're in harmony, anything is possible."

Chapter 11 The Mystery of the Glow
FLOATING FLIPPERS

After R. Mony safely secured Twinks and Nicci, she returned for me, and the two of us went back to the marina.

She led me directly to Sparrow's boat. Once there, she refused to leave, surfacing and submerging as if on a mission. As she rose, I saw barnacles on her back and smelled algae.

When she sank and rose again, I noticed hundreds of hairs all over her body, and I spotted the slashes. "You're showing me your scars, right?"

She squealed, and her flipper playfully grabbed me as she got closer so I could touch her. Her thick, wrinkled skin had a rough, leathery texture, and the scars were deeper than I thought they would be.

I scratched her a couple times, putting myself in her place. "I get it. The scars are from Buck's boat, and you want to get even," I said.

She applauded her tail on the waters.

I climbed aboard the boat, grabbed a flashlight, and took Sparrow's keys. When I edged back into the water, she was happy to see the keys.

"Now, let's go," I told her.

She refused.

"Show me what to do," I said.

Mony signaled me to sneak around to find out what was going on.

"Wish me luck," I whispered, wishing I had brought along a fingerprinting kit.

Soon I was alone. Snooping. I spied diving masks and fins lined up to dry. Boxes marked "labels" were stacked on a sailboat. Another boat stored brown and black plastic bags like the ones I saw Sparrow unload at the movies. A yacht was so full of stuff I thought it would sink.

I turned to leave. *Time to head home.*

Then it hit me. *Examine things up close.*

Silently, I sneaked up to the yacht, slipped over the railing, and ducked down behind a small lifeboat. No one could see me, but I could see and hear everything.

The first thing I heard was a whistle. It was a man crouched on the stern having a smoke and whistling. Quietly, I dove into the shadows where I listened to the creaking boat lines and watched the glowing ember until it disappeared. Then the man went inside the yacht.

Tiptoeing across the deck, I stuck my head into the air scoop to hear if anyone else was onboard. A slapping sound smacked over and over again, followed by thumping noises.

The Mystery of the Glow

Smack. Smack. Thump.

Smack. Smack. Thump.

I looked down the scoop to see what was happening and saw nothing but smelled a damp, earthy odor.

Every now and then, there was laughter. That chilled me to the bone. After all, I was alone and many were down there laughing. One had Hammer's voice. What were they doing?

Leave, the smart voice in my head pleaded.

Find out, the impulsive part of my brain said.

Creeping across the deck, I tripped over a coiled line and bumped into a box stored by the starboard rail. I froze in place, tasting the tangy salt air. It was eerie hiding in the shadows.

Rubbing my banged knee, I looked to see if anyone was coming. All I heard were muffled voices. The lights reflected on a porthole as I stood there staring at the boxes.

Finally, I dug through a box marked "Hammer's Labels." It wasn't easy yanking off the shipping tape and tugging the cardboard until my fingers bled, but it finally opened.

The labels inside read: "HAMMER IT HOME FERTILIZER. Prevents algae and red tide. Use as much as you want during rainy season."

"Hammer's helping our environment," I whispered to myself.

But deep in my gut, I knew that wasn't true. So I slithered over to the porthole to peek. I saw five men working.

There was a big man at the end of a long table. He got a black and brown plastic bag, placed it on the table, and carefully lined up a shiny, new label. He smoothed the label precisely in the center of the bag, took his palm, and smacked it in place. Then he stacked the bag in the corner.

Smack. Smack. Thump.

Smack. Smack. Thump. Bag after bag.

Hammer was relabeling.

The damp, earthy smell was from fertilizer! I thought.

The porthole was open, so I heard them.

"What a great scam," Hammer laughed. "We're selling fertilizer to use during rainy season. Most of it washes away, so we get to sell it again and again to the same suckers."

"Hammer, how did you come up with this idea?" a loud guy laughed.

"I saw it on the news. Big story on how our waterways get polluted. And, as usual, I found a way for *me* to benefit," Hammer said.

"What did they say?" the big man asked.

"There's a ban of fertilizing during rainy season because the nitrogen and phosphorus get washed into the waterways, feeding algae and red tide. But I always seem to forget to mention these points in my sales pitch," Hammer boasted.

Everyone laughed.

"They said to limit the use of fertilizer in Southwest Florida during rainy season. They even had an ad—'Don't Feed the Monster,' " Hammer added.

"Monster?"

"The slime. All that toxic runoff feeds the algal blooms. Hey, I can't worry about the whole world," Hammer smirked as he stepped outside of the room. "But I always take care of number one." He pointed to himself.

After Hammer left, the others hooted. The loud guy said, "Hammer sticks on phony labels with the wrong instructions."

Hammer's the real monster!" I thought.

"No wonder he sells so much," one bragged.

"Hammer's a thief!" I gasped. "He gets people to fertilize the wrong way and ruins our waters."

I have to do something. But what?

It didn't matter. I wouldn't get the chance. As I turned, Hammer stood behind me, fuming with anger. He seized my arm and yanked me away from the porthole.

"I tied you up. Why are you here?" he growled.

He shoved me toward the boxes. Big mistake. I reached out and tugged on some of them until the whole pile crashed on Hammer's head.

He sure knows bad language. As he screamed, I raced to the boat's ignition, pulled out the key, scrambled down the ladder, and sprinted away.

In the distance I saw R. Mony's glow moving close to the barge that Twinks had untied. Her clue!

By then, all of the workers were on deck.

The big guy noticed the barge, too. "Stop the kid!" he shouted. Racing after me, he stumbled over the boxes that held the masks and flippers, knocking them into the water.

Hammer tried to start the yacht, but there was no key. Sparrow tried to start his boat. No key.

When the barge moved close to land, I raced to the end of the pier and signaled with my flashlight. As the barge passed by, I hopped over the water and onto it, holding the flashlight high over my head like the Statue of Liberty.

The Mystery of the Glow

Looking back, I saw the entire place in chaos. Hammer and Buck jumped on an inflatable, paddled through the turquoise and neon pink flippers that were floating in the river, and raced north toward the Cape Coral Bridge.

THE DISPLAY

As the barge moved away from the pier, the three of us clapped.

"Group hug!" I shouted.

Twinks cheered, "Everyone, give it up for Mony!"

"Hey, everyone, give it up for Mony! Put your hands in the air and give it up for her," Nicci said. She put those words into a musical chant, and we three sang it over and over.

We were a bright, sunny Saturday after a long, rainy week. So rad.

"That was phenomenal!" Nicci said.

"Out of bounds," Twinks said. Then he yelled, "Look over there."

And we watched Hammer and Buck escape. Boy, were they rattled.

"Some poor boater won't see the inflatable in the dark and figure a hammerhead shark is coming right at him," Nicci giggled.

"Hammer sure looks like one," we agreed.

"Except the shark is better looking," Twinks said.

"And Buck is a turtle pulling his head in to hide from the world," Nicci added.

Next we scouted every inch of the old barge and found the fireworks.

We got to work and set them up to alert the cops to come to our rescue. The fireworks shot high in the sky and separated into five or six smaller ones. Ruby red, sapphire, and silver fireworks burst overhead.

BANG!

"Ohhhhhhhhh," Nicci said.

"Ahhhhhhhhhhhhh," Twinks joined.

BOOM!

Reflecting in the display, Mony raised her flipper for a high five. "We make a great team," I told her.

"Whoever heard of a glow leading a takedown?" Twinks laughed.

Mony squealed as we lit another firework which bulleted the heavens, spraying gold dust on the target below.

"Ohhhhhhhhhhhhhhh," Sparrow yelled.

"Ahhhhhhhhhh," the men cried when they heard the sirens and saw the red flashing lights of the police cars swarming the yacht club.

BOOM!

"The fireworks worked; they led the cops right to them," Nicci said.

"Yeah, J. R. was right when he said that Mony had a plan," Twinks agreed.

A strange thing happened. Twinks and Nicci saw it too. Mony intentionally came up under one of the masks and balanced it on her face. The last time we saw her that night she was frolicking down the river wearing it.

And I swear I saw a neon pink flipper attached to her tail.

THE GOOD AND THE BAD

The law couldn't find Hammer or Buck. Mony could have told where they were hiding, but no one asked her. They grilled us kids and said they'd get our phones back to us when they found them.

Luckily, we didn't have to testify, and no charges were filed against us. I told the police to call me if they ever ran a sting on some other dope like Hammer.

Maybe I should put up a sign: soccer player by day; detective by night, I thought.

The Florida Law Enforcement guys couldn't believe Hammer sank so low as to put phony labels on those bags of fertilizer. They agreed he should get slammed in the slammer.

But what about the bigger problems? The lousy water management. Who's going to fix that????

One of the men was a cool dude who took the time to fill us in. He told us that the Herbert Hoover Dike around Lake O is old and stressed. Their area could flood, so when the water gets too high, they release some of it.

"The dike was made from shells, sand, and gravel, so it can breach," he said.

I need to learn more about this, I thought.

"The problem is that the sugar farms use lake water and then pump it, polluted, *back* into the lake," he explained.

"That's awful," I said.

"Here's the zinger," the dude added. "The gates are near the bottom, so polluted muck comes down the Caloosahatchee River instead of the cleaner water at the top."

"Nobody wants dirty water," I said.

"We need to restore the natural flow," he added.

The big question is who decides what to do? The Army Corps? The Water District? The courts? Florida's best scientists?

No matter who has the power, they must remember our west coast of Florida.

"Some years have too much rain; some don't," he explained.

Mr. Cool Dude said that *dry* conditions also affect everything. "That's why we're building the C-43 reservoir to hold water, so we can clean and release it during dry spells to prevent our river from getting too salty," he continued.

If the cool dude ever ran for office, I told him I'd run his campaign. Then I exclaimed, "Farmers and big shots must *take action!*"

"The dike must be fixed fast!!!" he agreed. "It's a danger to people and to the environment."

The Mystery of the Glow

As Twinks filled in paper work, Nicci and I were by ourselves on the barge. We laughed about Sparrow's arrest.

"Wasn't Mony nifty in the fins and mask?" I asked.

"She was brilliant. J. R., she changed our lives."

More than you'll ever know.

"I hope we catch Hammer; he's rotten," she said. "Red tide does happen naturally, but it is also a result of runoff, and that's why Hammer was wrong. So wrong."

"So is anyone who throws our eco-system off balance," I said.

Nicci gave a big smile and said, "How true! I'm a Libra. The Libra scales represent justice, and I can really feel it when things are off balance. After all the things I have learned lately, my scale is so far off balance, I feel like I might tip right over."

She pretended she was tipping over.

"What's your sign, J. R.?" she continued.

"Sign?"

"Zodiac sign. When were you born?"

"February 14th."

"You're a valentine?" she giggled.

"I hope you're not going to give me all those stupid cupid jokes," I said.

"Heck, no," she answered. "But it's so perfect you won't believe it. February is Aquarius—the water bearer!"

Water? That is amazing, I thought.

"And I read that Aquarians can be late in arriving since time means nothing to them," she added.

Well, I finally arrived and better late than never, I reasoned.

The full moon seemed to skate across the top of the water. I pointed at it.

"Oh, I knew it was a full moon, all right," she said. "I can feel a full moon coming long before it's in the sky."

"You can?"

"I'm a writer and a full moon stirs my creative juices," she added.

"What do you write?" I asked.

"Songs, poems, and stories about saving the environment. Once, I wrote a play about Homer's *Odyssey* that you'd swear Twinks wrote because it has so many puns in it," Nicci said.

"What do you do with things you write?" I wondered.

"They are all part of my dream. J. R., did you ever read the poem 'Dream Deferred' by Langston Hughes?"

"No."

"He asks about the dreams we have that are never fulfilled but are put off or postponed to a later time. He wonders what happens to them when they are set aside. Where do you think they go?" she asked.

"I have no idea."

"Do you write?" she asked.

"Only my name on checks," I laughed.

Me? A writer? What could I ever write about except this thing about Buck and Hammer and the water management and Mony and my fears? But no one would believe it, I thought.

Nicci interrupted my thoughts. "Those hyacinth plants aren't the only delicate thing. So is Mony." She hesitated, then added softly, "And your heart."

"You're delicate, too," I said.

"Is that right?" she snickered.

"You're special, Nicci. Compassionate, fun, brave," I said.

"You're cool yourself, J. R."

"Delicate," I repeated, relishing the total karma of the moment. The world stood still. Silence exploded from the skies and stars seemed to crash on my head. It was the kind of moment that signals everything is all right in the world—like a soda feels when it has its fizz.

As we sat there, I glanced down into the dark waters. Bubbles danced to the surface. I knew R. Mony was nearby.

"HARMONY," the bubbles said, "PURE HARMONY!!!!"

CHAPTER TWELVE

The Calm Before The Storm

What could be worse than Hammer and Buck still running loose? That gave me the creeps. Not that we didn't try to locate them. The cops combed the city. Mony and I searched the waterways. But those two jerks had disappeared.

Finally, I gave up worrying about Hammer and decided I'd rather talk with Mony about life. Those days were peaceful. Little did I know that the worst was yet to come. Little did I suspect that I was in the eye of a hurricane.

One day, Mony got silly. When I read her message, I laughed as hard as any kid could. It simply read, "#KnockKnock."

"Hash tag?" I laughed. "You're certainly getting modern."

She surfaced and exhaled.

"Twinks will love that you are telling knock-knock jokes," I said into the system.

She snorted and I chuckled.

Then, Mony got personal. "Are you and Nicci an item?" Her words appeared on the screen.

"We're friends," I said.

"Sometimes friends get close like a family." Mony's words came up to the computer screen as red letters..

I explained that all my aunts and uncles live up north, and I had seen none of them since moving to Cape Coral.

"You have your mom and your dad," R. Mony told me.

"Yeah, but when they separated, they took a chunk of me. I feel like the divorce is my fault," I said.

"That's ridiculous. Your parents are adults; they had their relationship before you even came along. Stop feeling guilty about something you didn't cause," she explained.

"Mony, you can do all sorts of things. Get them together."

"J. R., divorce is never easy. They got rid of all of their problems, didn't they? Yes, but now they have a whole bunch of different ones."

"I hoped…"

"No, J. R., when we talk of harmony, I mean all of nature. It's not up to me to deal with individual parts. It's up to them." Her words moved across the screen.

"Are you sure?" I asked.

"It's all much more complicated than we could cover in a five minute talk, but the important part right now is to stop blaming yourself."

"Mony, it sounds as if you've given this thought," I said into the system.

"Lately, I've given *family* lots of thought," she answered.

"Why?"

"Because I'm going to have a baby!" she told me.

"A baby?" I did a flip. "Hear that, world? I'm gonna be an uncle!"

CHAPTER THIRTEEN

Tricked

I always go to Coach Eddie's soccer camps at Cape Coral High School. Hundreds of kids attend because it's everything we love about soccer, and we even get to swim. Plus they always have freeze pops.

I grabbed all my soccer stuff and jumped on my bike. When I got there, I was amazed that Twinks wasn't on the field; he never missed a camp before.

Coach Eddie played professional soccer for ten seasons, and he's cool. He had it set up so we had to pass the ball four times without an opponent touching it before we could shoot on goal. This drill is important because possession is the key to soccer–if the other team can't take the ball from you, they can't score.

I wish Twinks came; he'd love this, I thought, expecting him to rush into position any minute. Twinks knew it was the CCSA's 40th anniversary, and Coach Eddie even had his brother Mike as a guest coach.

Twinks! What's wrong? Where is he?

I left the field and sped to Twinks' house to find out why he'd skip a soccer camp. No one was home.

I had gotten my phone back from the police, but it was turned off during soccer, so I flipped it on. It was bulging with texts from Twinks about seeing me in a hurry. And a phone message from Hammer that said to meet him at Four Freedoms Park.

I sent a text to Twinks, telling him where I was going and beat it to the park to wait for Hammer. As I walked through the gate, I spotted the word "Danger" that some kids had scribbled with chalk on the decking for a game they made up, but there was no Hammer.

"J. R., over here!" someone yelled. It was three kids I know from soccer—Vincent, Bailey, and Emily—who were by the picnic tables juggling soccer balls. I motioned that I was a guy on a mission, but I figured I'd keep those three in mind in case Hammer got rough with me.

Why does Hammer want to meet me? I thought while noticing an eagle overhead.

For over an hour, I looked for him. As I circled the rocking horse, rocking frog, and slides, I watched a carefree mother push her two little kids, Tai and Trinity, on a tire swing.

But no sign of Hammer.

I shot off another text to Twinks and strolled over to the nearby basin. Standing on a bush was a Great White Egret with its head bobbing and swaying back and forth until its pointed beak speared a small lizard. I figured I had a lot in common with that little lizard.

From shore, I scanned the water for Hammer and spotted nine or ten anchored sailboats. Carefully, I stared at each boat to see if any of them could be Hammer's manufacturing company.

But no.

This wasn't working. It was time for some common sense before Hammer hurt someone, so I started for a nearby bank to ask them if I should call the police.

Then I saw him racing toward me.

Twinks.

"J. R., you're O.K."

"Of course I am."

"You must run home," Twinks warned me. "It's the same trick they used on me. Hammer said to meet and then sneaked in my house and ransacked my things."

"Is he nuts? Let's get to my house fast," I said.

We raced to my house. Too late. My room was never neat, but this was a disaster. My closet avalanched into the room, and drawers dripped with soccer shorts, socks, and shin guards. Dangling from the fan, my underwear whirled overhead. Cyclone soccer cards and computer printouts of our inventions were all over the room.

"Oh, no," I cried, sifting through our records of Mony's existence tossed around the room like garbage. "They've seen everything, Twinks, and know about Mony! They'll find her, and who knows what they'll do to her. We have to warn her. Now!"

I bent and raked up pieces of a ripped picture—a shot of gentle, passive Mony happily munching water hyacinths. My eye caught one word lit up on the computer screen that said it all.

SAVE.

ENTANGLED

We had to warn R. Mony, so we zoomed to the yacht club and jammed on the equipment. Mony responded immediately.

"You're in danger," I told her.

"True, but I think you mean 'endangered'," she replied.

"Everything was in my computer," I said.

"Don't worry. Technology and nature can live in harmony," Mony answered.

I got to the point and explained how Hammer had broken in my room and knew about her, and she had to go away.

"Away?"

"Yes, they'll hurt you," I said.

"I won't go," Mony said.

As her words came across the screen, I saw them–Buck and Hammer sneaking up behind her on a boat. It was too late to warn poor Mony.

"Leave her alone!" I screamed.

"Don't touch her," Twinks added.

As he spoke, some men placed a giant sling around her, loaded her aboard, and sprayed her skin moist as she settled on foam bedding on the boat.

Her glow flickered.

"She's just a manatee. What do you want with a manatee?" I screamed.

"Nothing with a regular one, but this one will make us rich. We'll rent her for big bucks," Hammer growled.

"No one rents manatees," I said.

"Her powers could be used in drug deals or a world takeover. She could spy, control nuclear subs, or be a weapon herself. Who cares which side she's on, we'll get rich," Hammer sneered.

"No, please," I cried.

R. Mony fluttered like a magnificent butterfly trapped in a spider web. In anguish she groaned a pathetic moan like a cow being milked.

She was captured!

CHAPTER FOURTEEN

Mony's Message

As the bruised skies of night were healed by dawn, I still hadn't slept. By the time Twinks and I quit looking, I couldn't sleep because my mind was racing.

For years I was like the bubble gum in the water fountain at school—stuck in place and drowning. Then Mony came along.

Now she got snatched away and I missed her; I wanted to tell her that I felt better since our talks. At least I understood why I felt guilty.

I wanted to thank her for showing me the big picture. It wasn't such a mystery, after all. The answers were there the whole time. Sometimes, though, we don't miss the glow until it's gone.

Little by little, my stomach settled. Finally, I trudged out to the kitchen to reheat leftovers from Chen's. After sipping steaming wonton soup, I started feeling like my old self and polished off some Moo Shu Pork with pancakes. Fortune cookies were in the bag, but I was afraid to open them. Afraid to read my own fortune.

Slowly, I was feeling human again, and I reached for the newspaper, headed to my room, and flopped back on my bed across my skinny pillow. After scanning the cartoons, I filled in all of the easy answers on the crossword puzzle.

I couldn't believe it. On the crossword puzzle, one across said that "over 800 died in Florida waters last year," and "manatees" was the answer.

A feature article about the soccer camp in the "Sports Section" caught my attention. Scores and the coming schedule for the Cyclones were listed, too, and then I saw something on the bottom of the page that made my eyes pop.

A message from Mony.

"DELICATE. R. MONY," it read.

Mony had put a clue in the newspaper! But what?

Being a mammal, she was probably barely alive and being taken to Hammer's hideout. Desperate. Lost. In shock. Searching for something familiar.

Then she saw the water hyacinth plants. Seeing them saddened her because she would never munch

The Mystery of the Glow

them again. In a final attempt to survive, she mustered up every ounce of strength to summon her forces to beam one last message.

To the world. To anyone who would listen.

I pictured her message lifting out of the canal and beaming onto the only computer operating late at night. It wasn't ours. It lit a nearby office—the computerized system of the *Daily Breeze,* Cape Coral's newspaper. The monitor snatched the airborne message frequencies, sorted, and placed them in the news.

A huge machine spit out the next day's paper. Copy after copy flipped from its jaws, printing it over and over again:

DELICATE. R. MONY.

DELICATE. R. MONY.

Flying across the room, I grabbed my phone, texted Twinks, and told him I knew where Mony was.

"Where?" Twinks texted back.

"I don't know the exact spot."

"J. R., you got to be kidding. The Caloosahatchee not only connects to the Gulf of Mexico, but it's part of the Intracoastal Waterway that runs from New Jersey to Texas. Our city has more than 400 miles of canals—that's more than Venice, Italy," Twinks' text said. "You must be more exact."

"She's somewhere between Caloosa Middle School and the *Breeze* newspaper. She's probably on the east side of Del Prado by some water hyacinths," I typed.

"Wow! I'll get my boat and be there pronto!"

GIVING UP

By the time we got there, a heavy fog draped over the area, and the clouds looked like a giant, grey tie-dyed shirt. Even though we could barely see past the front of the boat, we searched every inch near the *Breeze*. Right when I wanted to give up, Twinks spied hyacinth plants along the edge of a wide canal.

Somehow we knew it was the spot. Quietly edging toward it, we discovered boards blocking the end of the canal. As I climbed out of Twinks' boat to remove the homemade gate, Twinks coughed, "I hope this isn't where they hid her. There's red tide trapped in there."

We saw R. Mony. Motionless.

I cried, "She warned us that people need to care or she'd be gone…forever!"

But why?

Selfishness?

Greed?

Ignorance?

Couldn't they see past that into tomorrow?

Reaching through the red tainted water, we caressed her still body, remembering her talks and dreams.

"Maybe it's not too late," we sighed.

Staggering forward, I stroked the polluted water from her eyes and whispered hope to her being. Caressing Mony's leathery body, I patted her scarred back and embraced her mucky flippers and told her that she was the most magnificent of all beings.

Mony's button eye twitched, looking like a raisin pressed deeply in the Pillsbury dough boy.

"She's alive!" we cheered.

We nudged her toward the open waters.

She tried to move but couldn't. Too sad. Too exhausted.

"Please, Mony. Try," I urged, lovingly spraying water over her being. I picked a water hyacinth. "Here. Your favorite."

She ignored the flower.

"Don't you remember a 'delicate'?"

Of course she did. It was her nature—delicate and fragile. Didn't we understand?

That is the problem.

A huge fluorescent tear rolled from her tiny, beady eye as I cried, "Mony, I LOVE YOU!"

Maybe that wasn't enough. Was loving something enough? Was thinking it was beautiful enough?

Perhaps it would take more than that.

The Mystery of the Glow

I looked into Mony's eye; it was flat, like peering into the sky after someone had ripped away the stars. "Mony, it's up to you."

Is it? Somehow I don't think so. And maybe it's not worth the price.

Mony groaned. It was more than a groan of pain. It was a groan of the ages—past and future. It was the groan of a broken heart.

Slowly, R. Mony moved toward the Gulf of Mexico, but she didn't swim like her playful, contented self. Her blank eyes and broken heart told it all.

CHAPTER FIFTEEN

Justice At Last

Shoulders sagging, we got on the boat to leave. "Why are some people mean to animals?" Twinks asked.

I agreed and then whined how Hammer's fertilizer contributed to the algae that hurt people and Mony. "You know, Twinks, we have enough problems with our waters without having someone ruin them on purpose. That's why I'm so mad. Hammer must pay."

It didn't take us long to figure out which house was his—it was on a canal near where we found Mony. Hammer's boat was tied to a dock.

Twinks hid his boat nearby.

"He will pay when we use this," I said, lugging our VR game out of the cabin.

"*King?* We're taking our VR game?" Twinks wondered. "Why?"

The Mystery of the Glow

"You'll see."

"It's like having our own King Kong along," Twinks laughed.

I said to grab some ropes and a tetherball.

"We also need this." I gathered up the remote control and the drone. Quickly, I hooked a fishnet to the bottom of the drone.

"The drone? It's never been tested for something like this," Twinks said. "What if things go wrong?"

"No way; we're too good. Remember Amazon and Dominoes hope to have drone deliveries someday. We might just beat them to it."

We set up the drone so it was ready to fly at a moment's notice and placed it on the deck of the boat. "Are we ready for takeoff?" Twinks asked as he saluted me.

"We are so ready," I said.

"Wow, we're going to fight Hammer with our VR game *and* the drone. I'm actually speechless," Twinks said.

Hard to believe Twinks didn't even spit out a knock-knock joke.

THE GAME

The sun was burning a hole in the fog as we sneaked up to Hammer's house. Silently, we crept toward it, peeked in a window, and spotted Buck sleeping. Twinks said to get him, but it was Hammer we wanted.

"Remember, Twinks, stay hidden in the closet," I whispered.

We slipped through a sliding door into Hammer's bedroom. Twinks tied the tetherball to the ceiling fan, and I stretched the ropes across the room. Cautiously, I reached for Hammer's head to put the goggles on him, but he flipped over.

"Buck, that you?" he called as I dropped under the bed. After a few minutes, I sneaked out and slipped the virtual reality goggles over his ruffled hair and the gloves with special electronic sensors on his hands.

"What's going on?" he moaned as he stood up in his pink and white pajamas.

I clicked on the remote control for the VR game. I knew what Hammer was seeing—a 3D make-believe soccer field with him inside the net as the goalie. No matter what Hammer did, he would feel the shots.

Since we were outside the goggles, he wouldn't see us.

The Mystery of the Glow

"We're going to shoot balls at you. If you don't duck, it will hurt," I yelled.

Twinks popped out of the closet and called, "Over here." As Hammer lumbered toward his voice, Twinks gave a wink, a knock-knock, and said it was "Justin."

"Justin who?" I asked.

"Justin time to see Hammer learn to be a goalie," Twinks laughed.

I snapped the button that says "Shoot on Goal" and shouted, "Here comes a shot, Hammer."

Hammer bent. I smirked. He thought the balls were actually coming at him.

"Here's another one," I called as Hammer dove across the room, kicking the air. He bobbed and weaved. I knew it stung as ball after ball smashed him because a soccer ball can come at you at 75 miles per hour, and the game felt real.

"This hurts. Ouch. My head," he bawled and punched the air.

I recalled how rattled I got when I was in the game, but from the outside it was hilarious to watch.

Buck stormed into the room and asked what was going on; we said Hammer flipped his lid. Buck pounced on my back, drooled on my hair, and gripped me like a cape. I swirled around in frantic circles, hoping he'd let go.

As I whirled, his feet smashed against Hammer. Unable to see what was happening, Hammer lashed out until he grabbed Buck's flying ankles and yanked them until Buck stretched across the room like a giant piece of bubble gum, snapped, and crashed to the floor.

Awkwardly, Buck pushed up to a standing position. The front of his messy hair stood straight up, and he kept shoving it to the side.

"I'm outa here," Buck said as he bolted out of the house, cramming stuff into a bag like a kid with a backpack when the bell rings. Well, school was out for Buck!

As he fled, Buck's appearance changed—no longer a fierce, oppressive bully but more like a distorted reflection in a fun house mirror. A cracked one.

Our attention returned to Hammer. "You're next. We will slam you unless…"

"Unless what?"

"You confess to the cops," I said.

"To what?" Hammer blubbered.

"Ruining the environment with your fertilizer scam," I answered.

"No."

I pushed buttons marked "Faster" and "More Powerful." It didn't take long for the game to go out of control. Soccer balls pounded everywhere.

The Mystery of the Glow

Players had good form—head down, eyes on the ball, follow through, and they blasted Hammer almost simultaneously, showering him with forceful shots from every direction.

Head balls.

Low ones.

Chip and placement shots.

Forty yard thunderbolts.

Hammer was bombarded with shots that zoomed across the grass and soared to the goal with lightning speed. Blasts of power smacked him. I couldn't decide if he was attacking or hiding as he swooped, veered to the right, and twisted to the left.

THUD! The kicks were so loud that we heard them from outside of the game as Hammer tumbled and stumbled across the room.

THUMP!

SLAM!

A player charged the keeper, studs up. But there was no whistle. Nothing. Not even a foul. "Play on," the virtual referee said.

All the while players struck their laces on the sweet spots for maximum power over and over with such force that Hammer flipped and tripped over the furniture.

WAM! Duck. Stagger. WHACK!

I pushed all the buttons at once. A plethora of balls flew at Hammer, and he looked like a stuntman in a movie.

I signaled Twinks to punch the tetherball dangling from the fan, and it flew across the room, slamming Hammer over and over again. Now he was not only getting smashed from the game itself but also from the ball outside of it.

Twinks' voice came from every direction, taunting Hammer with knock-knock jokes.

"Who's there?" I asked.

"One," Twinks said.

"One who?" I wondered.

"One some more, Hammer?" Twinks laughed.

BAM! Hammer clumsily got tangled in the ropes that were strung all around the room. He howled bad words, danced on his toes, and tumbled over the ropes.

As we say in soccer, he was in the zone.

He did a *chilena*. Imagine seeing a goalie do the bicycle kick against himself. I laughed hard.

He zigzagged across the hall, slammed against the couch, knocked the flat screen TV off the wall, and crashed to the floor. As Hammer violently shook his head to clear his mind, he hammered his chin on the edge of a desk.

The goggles fell off and flew through the air.

Hammer was free from the VR game. Boy, was he surprised to see us. "So it was you!"

"Yup," Twinks said, strutting up to Hammer. "How about you and I take a selfie?" Leaning in toward Hammer's shoulder, Twinks raised his phone and took their picture.

"You two are nuts!" Hammer shouted, bolting toward the door.

"He's getting away!" Twinks moaned.

"No. I have a trap outside," I said.

I flipped on the remote control and dialed the drone app. The flight control hardware took over. In a jiffy, our drone lifted off Twinks' boat and whirled directly overhead.

"Help!" Hammer yelled as the drone cast a glaring light in his eyes. The dazzling beam was so intense that he squinted and tried to figure out what was happening.

The drone buzzed above Hammer's head and hovered there as he cowered and clapped both hands over his ears to block the whirring sound. The closer it got, the more he cringed.

Click! Click! The camera took a video of Hammer flinching and posted it on YouTube.

Hammer yelled, "What is that thing? What's happening?"

I pushed a secret button. The drone zoomed in closer and dropped the net which plunged over Hammer's entire body. Crash! Bam! Zing!

He spread out his arms, but they got snarled. Stretched his legs, but they got tangled. It tied around him like we had caught a huge fish. He was captured!

"I'm trapped!" he cried.

"Now you know how Mony felt," I snarled.

Hammer begged, "Stop! I'll talk."

Twinks slammed him on a lawn chair as I dialed 911 and smashed the phone to Hammer's ear. "I did it!" he confessed. "I'm guilty of ruining the water with algae. I hurt manatees. Come get me before these kids kill me!"

Twinks and I looked at each other and spoke at the same time. "Now, that's what I'm talking about!"

Then Twinks flashed a victory sign and said, "Knock. Knock."

"Who's there?" I chanted.

"Justice. Justice as it should end for anyone mean to R. Mony," Twinks added.

The police sirens blasted louder as they got closer and closer. Police raced toward Hammer and handcuffed him as I said, "Welcome to reality, virtually speaking."

The captain shouted at Hammer, "How dare you harm our water!"

Hammer bellowed, "Me? What about the politicians who don't take action? The sugar interests? The toxins released downstream? The Army Corps of Engineers?"

The cop didn't budge. "I'm talking about *you*! Not caring about algae as long as you make money. Red tide kills manatees and fish. Now get moving."

Another cop trudged toward us, yanking Buck up the canal bank. Shoulders sagging, Buck slinked toward us with his wet, flat hair covering his eyes. "He was hiding in the water in all that red tide. What do you think these dudes were up to?"

The captain answered. "Who knows? Only the birds and fish do, and they'll never tell. You know that animals can't communicate."

CHAPTER SIXTEEN

Searching For Harmony

Life *is* a roller coaster, and I was feeling both the ups and the downs. A party was in my head, celebrating Hammer's capture, while my heart beat a sad song, missing Mony.

We searched for Mony. Finally, we went home and sat silently in sadness.

Until I started laughing. There's something weird about me; when I've been sad for a long time, a switch turns on, and I get silly. "Hammer looked hilarious in our game," I said. "The only thing missing was the mud."

"J. R., imitate Hammer," Nicci said.

With eyes shut, I said, "Is this a table?" Then flipped over it.

Twinks held a pretend microphone and asked me, "Hammer, how do you feel?"

The Mystery of the Glow

"Ouch. It hurts," I mimicked Hammer.

Nicci giggled. "I love your VR game for the goalie who rules."

"Cops rule; crooks drool," Twinks said.

"Step outside under the spotlight, Hammer. Watch out for falling nets," I warned. "Ooops, here comes one."

"The game said you'd be *in a net,* Hammer," Nicci said with a big tee-hee.

"Forgive us if we 'drone' on," Twinks chuckled.

As we waved goodbye to a pretend Hammer, Twinks said, "We must make like lightning and bolt."

"Like a banana and split," I added.

"Like a dog and flea," Nicci snickered.

Then I got serious and said, "Hammer's small potatoes compared to the huge fight in front of us."

"Yes, the fight for clean water and for manatees!" Nicci said.

"Manatees?"

"Mony!!!" we all exclaimed.

"Let's get back to the yacht club!" I said, and we gathered all our stuff and scurried to the pier.

As we set up the computer, I ranted about manatees. How Columbus thought they were mermaids. How one named Chessie once swam from Florida to Rhode Island.

I spoke of the enemies of sea cows—algae, cold, loss of sea grass.

Red tide.

Boats.

As I spoke, we got a surprise. The monitor lit up.

"Hi,"

"Mony!" we yelled. "You're O.K."

"It was no picnic," she admitted.

"We thought you had given up," I said.

"I had until a miracle happened. And here she is." A 40 pound grey manatee broke the water's surface.

"A baby!" we cried.

"When I left, I was in the hands of man, and mankind was not being very kind. I was sad until I had a miracle." Mony's words crossed the screen.

"Her name?" I asked.

"Morrow. Tomorrow is what it's all about," Mony answered.

I peered into R. Mony's eyes. They were no longer blank and flat and empty; they sparkled as if the stars had been sewn back into the skies.

"You kids, Morrow, and I will have fun."

"No. You must leave," I told her.

"Will we meet again?" she asked.

"Perhaps. But until man can live in harmony with nature, it is the only way. Thanks for teaching us your secret," I said into the system.

"It's no secret. It was there all along," she answered.

"Take action," I agreed.

"Above all, you *must* convince your leaders that they are running out of time!" Mony said.

"We will."

"This dream cannot be deferred," she warned.

"We promise."

There was a long, empty silence. A fluorescent tear floated on the surface, and Mony sent up a message: "O. K., we'll go."

"Goodbye," I said into the system.

"NEVER say goodbye. GOODBYE IS FOREVER!" Mony's words turned the screen green.

"So long. We love you, and we love harmony," we said.

"HA**RMONY**! That's what it's all about," she answered.

"We will look for you," we said.

"If I lose my power and become a regular manatee again, I will still look for you. I'll be there. Things will happen in the oceans when you least expect them. Realize it is me still at work," Mony told us.

"We'll fight for you and your home," I promised.

Gulping to regain her composure, R. Mony motioned to Morrow. With a final flipper wave, they swam majestically toward the sea.

VIRTUAL REALITY

Twinks, Nicci, and I scurried down the dock, hoping to catch a last glimpse of our friends bravely swimming out to sea. When Mony gave her final glance, she saw the three of us embracing and waving, looking like one being from a distance—united in love.

Suddenly, for reasons unclear to even myself, I reached out past the computer and picked up the virtual reality goggles and slipped them on Twinks, Nicci, and me.

To our utter surprise, there were no soccer players. Instead, we saw Mony and Morrow. In amazement, the three of us *entered* that world, gracefully moving through magnificent, clean water where whales sang and the rhythms of the past serenaded the future.

Twinks, Nicci, and I continued to interface with the game as we floated under the purple shadows of peace through rainbow secrets that were at the same time young and old, innocent and wise. Bubbles of suffering and hatred popped as springs of unity gushed forth. Gold dust sprinkled the velvety waters as dolphins and manatees and animals swirled with reflections of mankind through raining violets and the smell of ginger and the taste of sweet honey in perfect harmony.

CHAPTER SEVENTEEN

The End
(Or the beginning…)

I picked up my phone and changed the outgoing message to "Hi. This is J. R. Collins. Dad and I are out having a tasty crunchy grouper dinner with fresh veggies at the Prawnbroker Restaurant. Tomorrow, Mom and I are heading to the Keys; we have a lot to talk about.

Can't get back to you right now, so leave your message at the beep."

"Harmony!"

Epilogue

Here's Nicci's response to Langston Hughes.
Dream by Nicci Nash
What happens to a dream deferred?
It dangles loosely out in space,
Floating, floating, ever floating,
Always looking for its place.

It wanders through the jungles,
Stalking, stalking evermore,
Growling out in raging anger,
Creeping, creeping evermore.

What happens to a dream deferred?
It chills to ice or turns to stone,
Or erodes into a treeless dust bowl
Left behind when winds have blown.

What can it do when you have lost it?
It can never stop its cries,
Sitting on some distant shore
Begging for another try.

So if your dream is slipping from you,
Never let it walk alone.
Stretch yourself until you reach it,
It's the dearest thing you own.

"You miss 100 percent of the shots you never take." Wayne Gretzky.

And that is not only in sports. We can't win this one unless we all give it our best shot! J. R. Collins.

From The Author

Dedication

This book is dedicated to my family because I am so proud of them, to Nana for her storytelling, to Deb for the word, and to my husband Ed for his karma of love, humor, and zest for life.

Acknowledgments

Thanks, Ed, for being my thesaurus; Eddie Carmean and Debbie Green for knowing where and when to give a push, and Eddie for clarifying soccer terms; Sharon Barr, Brian Glass, Dianne Konkel, and Mike Carmean for helping; and Mike and Dan Blank for suggesting CreateSpace.

Note:
Teacher's Edition available with purchase of a class set. Contact us by email for details.

Made in the USA
Charleston, SC
18 October 2014